THE GIRLS
FROM GOLDEN TO GILMORE

THE GIRLS

FROM GOLDEN
TO GILMORE

STAN ZIMMERMAN

The Girls: From Golden to Gilmore

© 2023 by Stan Zimmerman

The events depicted in this book are based upon the author's memories of them, and any unwitting errors that may appear are the author's own. Some names and details have been changed to protect privacy.

Editors: Deborah Froese, Mary Menke, Stephanie Thompson
Cover and Interior Design: Emma Elzinga

Author Photo by Braden Davis

3 West Garden Street, Ste. 718
Pensacola, FL 32502
www.indigoriverpublishing.com

Ordering Information:
Quantity sales: Special discounts are available on quantity purchases by corporations, associations, and others. For details, contact the publisher at the address above.
Orders by US trade bookstores and wholesalers: Please contact the publisher at the address above.

Printed in the United States of America

Library of Congress Control Number: 2023915520
ISBN: 978-1-954676-60-2
eBook ISBN: 978-1-954676-61-9

First Edition

With Indigo River Publishing, you can always expect great books, strong voices, and meaningful messages. Most importantly, you'll always find . . . *words worth reading.*

CONTENTS

PREFACE

THE O.G. (ORIGINAL GIRLS)

Okay, let's play a little Family Feud. What do you think is the number one question people ask me when they find out I wrote for *The Golden Girls*?

Give up?

It's "How could you, as a man, and a very young one at that, have written for four older women?"

Picture it: 1985. Back then, if you were a writer, you were expected to write for all kinds of people, not merely for who you were or what your personal life experiences had been.

At one of my early drama classes, they taught us the Golden Rule: "Acting is reacting." That meant listening and observing others. We were told to sit and watch people in a mall. I'm not a big fan of shopping, but spying on strangers, that's a different story.

Years later, when I first started writing with Jim Berg, I suggested we go out in Manhattan, watch people from afar, and then ad-lib what we thought they were saying, letting our imaginations run wild. (We do it to this day, so don't get scared if you see us somewhere talking in strange voices.)

But observation is only part of the answer to the number one question. I attribute my talent for writing for women to growing up with three strong, smart women: my grandmother, my sister, and my mother. All were so vocal and opinionated, you never had to wonder where they stood on a subject. Without them, I wouldn't have the career I've been so lucky to experience or have met all the extraordinary women I've been so fortunate to work with.

That's why I dedicate this book to them: three extraordinary women in their own right.

My grandmother, known as Mama, was the "Rose Kennedy" of our family. Like John F. Kennedy's mother, Mama carried herself with grace, dignity, and a strong sense of right and wrong—usually with a long Virginia Slim cigarette at her fingertips. (She insisted she never inhaled, long before Bill Clinton stole that phrase from her.) I was fascinated by the bright red lipstick stain she left on the filters and the way she'd tap the long snake of ash into a glamorous glass ashtray.

Mama was born in Texas, but she seemed East Coast classy to me. She dressed to the nines in the latest ensemble from Bonwit Teller. Once they became permissible for women of her generation to wear, her outfit of choice became a smart pantsuit. She was a real fashion plate. I never saw her without makeup or without her beautiful silver hair perfectly teased. (Think: Rose Nylund's helmet of hair.)

Mama attended every play I performed in as a kid. Years later, even after I was working on *Golden Girls*, she gave me the same career advice whenever I saw her. She'd say: "Stanley, just get your foot in the door."

I responded, "Mama, my foot is in. Now, I need to get the rest of my body in as well." I'm still working on that.

Even though Mama smoked, ate red meat, and never exercised a day in her life, she lived to be 101. We have strong genes in my family.

My sister and grandmother were two peas in a pod. My sister is whip-smart, exceptionally creative, and very funny. I thought she should've been the family writer, but she chose a different path. She worked in human resources on Wall Street where she met her husband, got married, and started having children. She eventually decided to leave the rat race and become a full-time mom.

When my sister started having babies, I decided to forgo my

overseas traveling adventures and come East to be with them. I wanted her kids to know me as more than a once-a-year visitor at Thanksgiving. I'm glad I made that investment and really enjoy being their "Guncle."

My sister was a picky eater, and when she was about five or six, she'd sometimes refuse to go out for our weekly Sunday night dinner with our grandparents. Chinese food is the go-to for Jews on weekends and Christmas, so we'd usually end up at Wing Hong's on Ten Mile and Southfield Road.

She'd lock herself in her room, and I was sent to coax her out. My early storytelling techniques started by sitting on her bed and dreaming out loud. I'd make up stories about moving to Hollywood and becoming a wildly successful actor. I'd weave fantastical tales about being rich enough to build my own mansion in the Hollywood Hills. I'd engage her with questions like, "How many bedrooms should I have?" or "Should I have an indoor or outdoor pool?"

Soon she'd be laughing, eventually getting in the car, and then chowing down fried chicken while everyone else enjoyed egg foo young.

(These stories turned out to be not so fantastical. Not the actor part, but I am very fortunate to live in a beautiful, three-story home in the Hollywood Hills. Though far from a mansion, it does prove the power of positive thinking at an early age. Kids, start dreaming!)

Then there's my mom, Susanne. (With an *s*, not a *z*, as she always reminded people.) When we were growing up, my mom wasn't shy about expressing herself—especially when it came to my father. They had an extremely contentious separation and divorce when I was seventeen. Horrible, loud fights erupted, usually in front of us, always within earshot.

Once my father moved out of the house, my mother became very depressed. On some dark days, she'd leave the house in a huff and go driving. She was so upset, I was afraid she'd have an accident. I was relieved when I'd hear her keys in the front door. But then she'd retreat to her bedroom and hide under the covers with the blinds shut. Like I did with my sister on Chinese food Sundays, I'd go into my mother's bedroom and try to make her laugh. And also get her to think about creating a life after my father.

Fortunately, Mom found purpose. She returned to a local college, Lawrence Tech, to get an accounting degree. Thrilled to discover that she was smarter than all the young twenty-somethings in her class, she loved seeing their shocked faces when she told them she had three kids at home. The more my mom dove into discovering herself, the more I wanted to spend time with her.

She loved movies, as did I. She'd find an offbeat indie film for us to see instead of the latest blockbuster. One was Paul Mazursky's *Next Stop, Greenwich Village,* set in the 1960s and starring the late Lenny Baker. I looked a lot like Lenny Baker and could relate to his passion for acting and wanting to study theater in NYC. Playing his love interest was a very young Ellen Greene, who went on to star in *Little Shop of Horrors.* That movie had a big effect on me.

Seeing those movies with my mom opened my eyes to a world outside of Southfield, Michigan, a small suburb of Detroit.

LIFE BEFORE THE LANAI

Before *The Golden Girls*, I was so sheltered, I had no idea what a "lanai" was. I had no idea what a lot of things were. While most kids would play outside, I'd play inside. In my basement, to be more specific.

I'd corral the neighborhood kids into putting on plays down there. Once I felt we rehearsed enough for the big time, I found the nerve to ask Mrs. Golden, my second-grade teacher at John F. Kennedy Elementary, if we could present the play to our class. (Yes, that was really her name. Foreshadowing?)

Surprisingly, Mrs. Golden agreed, even without seeing the play. She must have had faith in me because she also called in the other second grade classes. We pushed aside the desks, and the kids sat crosslegged on the linoleum floor, anxiously waiting to be entertained.

I don't recall what the play was about, but it was met with enthusiastic applause and, of course, laughter. Mrs. Golden saw my theatrical potential. I guess she was technically my first "Golden Girl."

One day after school, Mrs. Golden called my house.

I picked up the mustard yellow wall phone in our kitchen. "Hello?"

"Mrs. Zimmerman?" she asked.

This was not the first time I experienced this particular embarrassment. I lowered my voice several octaves and responded, "Uh, no. This is Stan."

"Can I speak to your mom?" she asked.

I handed the phone to my mother and waited with bated breath to hear why she was calling. Was I in trouble? Actually, the opposite. Mrs. Golden was so impressed with my creativity and showmanship, she suggested my mother send me to Cranbrook Summer Theatre School (CTS) in Bloomfield Hills.

My mother immediately contacted the school. One problem: I was seven-and-a-half. Their age requirement was eight. But luckily, the owner, Mrs. Annetta Wonnberger, agreed to meet me in person. My first audition!

At the theater school, Mrs. Wonnberger took me by the hand and led me away for a private interview, leaving my mom anxiously waiting in the lobby. My heart was pounding. What would this strange, old woman ask me? What if she didn't like my answers? Or didn't like me?

She asked questions like, "Why do you want to be an actor?" "How are you with memorizing lines and taking direction?" "Can you handle rejection?"

A few minutes later, we emerged from her office.

I must've said the right things, because Mrs. Wonnberger looked at my mother and said, "We'll take him!"

Nervousness on the first day of camp changed to worry when I received my first script. I was cast as "The King" in *The Princess and the Pea*.

Mrs. Wonnberger's husband, Carl—also very old—wrote all the plays. They were extremely corny, in my humble opinion as a pint-sized theater critic. Far below the high quality I was used to with my own work in my basement with the neighborhood kids. Carl's plays were about kings and queens—and not the fun "RuPaul" kind.

I had to take matters into my own hands.

Unbeknownst to the Wonnbergers, I stuffed my king's costume to make myself fat and put on my father's large, white Jack Purcell sneakers. The minute I walked onstage, the audience roared with laughter.

It sent a jolt right up my spine. I'd found my home: the theater.

My mom was my biggest supporter. When I needed ballet shoes for the final production at the end of my first summer at Cranbrook, she bought them without hesitation. But she told me to hide the shoes under my bed and not mention them to my father. Already there was shame around what I loved to do. She didn't explain until many years later that she knew he wouldn't approve. She wanted to wait for him to find out once I was safely onstage wearing them, and he couldn't stop the play and drag his son home in embarrassment.

My second biggest fan was Shayna Silverman, the mother of my classmate Julie. The Silvermans lived across the street from us. I'd often cast Julie as the ingenue in my basement plays.

One hot August afternoon, the doorbell rang.

Mrs. Silverman was out of breath and seemed very excited.

Me: "I'll go get my mom."

"No," she said. "I came to see you!"

She waved a copy of the Detroit Free Press with a big picture of me accompanying an article about my upcoming performance at Cranbrook.

Mrs. Silverman said, "Can I have your autograph?!"

Finally, someone besides me understood I was destined for stardom. I guess you could say Shayna was the first "Zimmerfan" (a term coined by Andrew Leeds in song on my Bravo reality show, *Situation: Comedy*).

I thrived at Cranbrook and made friends with everyone. Campers, counselors, you name it. Mostly girls. I was celebrated for my talents, which was hard to wrap my tiny head around. So different from school. By the time I was thirteen and at Thompson Junior High, I was constantly bullied or ignored. Or worse, spat on. All because I didn't act like the other boys. I wasn't good at sports. My hair was a frizzy mess. And I had horribly crooked front teeth. Not a pretty picture.

I would hold off using the boys' room all day for fear of getting beat up in there. Each day after school, my mom would watch for the bus to pull up at the corner. Then she'd hold our front door open for me, so I could have a clear, unobstructed path to the toilet, knowing that every second counted.

After the bathroom, I'd hide in the safety of my jungle-themed bedroom, where I'd spend hours daydreaming. There, I created my own imaginary TV network with seven nights of programming. I even made a scheduling board out of cardboard and drew ads announcing my new fall lineup. I also created the Junior Emmy Awards show, the first award show given by kids. I invited the cast of *The Carol Burnett Show*. They never RSVP'd.

I let off steam by putting on my *West Side Story* LP and dancing a high-energy rendition of the song "Cool." My parents didn't know what I was doing upstairs in my bedroom, making so much racket. My poor mustard-and-orange-colored shag carpet was getting completely destroyed from me sliding on my knees at the end of the song.

My attempts to create an alternate reality in my room didn't alleviate the darkness. Adding to that, when I looked in the mirror, I didn't like what I saw. Behind closed doors, I quietly contemplated killing myself. I didn't want to go to school every day and face the constant torment. But I was too afraid of pain. I couldn't even swallow St. Joseph Children's Aspirin. Using dance again, I choreographed my funeral to another record, one I got for my bar mitzvah, The Moody Blues' esoteric album, *Days of Future Passed*. This musical number would play out in front of my junior high school at bus time, so my classmates would know what they'd driven me to.

When I got to Southfield High School, I used the backstage bathroom at the auditorium. It was safer. I'd also finally stopped my daily attempts to flatten my hair by squashing it under a ski cap at breakfast. (With the humidity in Michigan, it was completely frizzy by the time I got to school anyway.) In the summer between ninth and tenth grade, I let my hair go naturally wavy, into a "Jewfro," a term at the time.

I was suddenly popular. I attributed it to my new hairstyle. But I was still confused. Could kids really be that shallow?

Fortunately, theater came to my rescue again. As did three very influential female high school teachers. These women were quick to recognize that when it came to acting, I was not playing around. First, there was Gladys Bernstein, my tenth grade Play Production teacher. Mrs. Bernstein was a true New Yorker—accent and attitude. We'd talk endlessly about Broadway in her office. Like two grown-ups.

Mrs. Bernstein was so impressed with me that she recommended Virginia Borts, the main drama teacher, audition me for the fall production of *Cactus Flower*, even though I wasn't right for any of the parts. On audition night, I got a call at home.

Mrs. Borts: "I'm going to write a part in the play for you. A character that was in the movie. A persnickety record store manager." (I hope there's a statute of limitations because that's completely against play licensing rules.)

I was thrilled, even though I only had a few lines. And boy, did I milk them, getting laughs where there weren't any. Next cast as a dancer in the spring musical, *Anything Goes,* I made friends with many upperclassmen. I was so well-liked, I was voted President of our local Thespian Society Troupe for my senior year. I took that job seriously. Some thought too seriously. But theater wasn't simply something fun to do; it was my everything.

In high school, it became my morning ritual to head straight from the bus to our school auditorium to meet with the other "theater geeks." Most of my closest friends were again girls: Leslie Freedman, Tracy Dines, Beth Schwartz, Lisa Pulice, and Adrienne Foner. We'd hang out there until it was time to go to our first class, then meet up again for lunch. After school, we'd be there for rehearsals. It was our home away from home.

It was a good escape from my own home, where my parents' marriage was disintegrating. Back then, divorce was not commonplace, and when I heard they were splitting up, the main emotion I felt was embarrassment. Like my life had turned into one of those tragic, over-the-top ABC Movies of the Week. The only one I could confide in about all this turmoil was Virginia Campbell, our African American housekeeper. She was so easy to talk to and always had a sympathetic ear.

But onstage, I found solace. I could escape into the comedies of Neil Simon's *God's Favorite* and Kaufman and Hart's *You Can't Take it With You* or musicals like *Damn Yankees*. The bickering at home was replaced with laughter, creativity, and friendships I still have today.

I was also fortunate to spend two summers as a junior apprentice at Hampton Playhouse in Hampton Beach, New Hampshire, a summer theater camp that my cousin Don Epstein recommended.

At Hampton Playhouse, I made lots of friends; again, mostly girls: Joann Teitelbaum, Maria Manuche, Laura Spitzer, and Debbie Gardner. I also started to have feelings for boys. Especially one senior apprentice. He was a New York actor who played Jesus in the main stage's production of *Godspell*. I didn't waste my time with an apostle. I went right for the big guy!

I'd stare out my cabin room window as the object of my affection walked to the theater nightly in cutoff jean short shorts with a little fringe hanging down in all the right places. I knew those feelings I was having weren't accepted by society, so I did everything in my power to squash them.

At Hampton Playhouse, the first Saturday children's play was *Hansel and Gretel*. The head of the theater, John Vari, asked to see me privately. He walked me over to a big tree in front of the main office so we could talk privately. I was nervous. Did I do something wrong? Am I the worst actor ever? Was I being sent home early? He chose his words carefully. "We want to cast you as the witch," he said, blinking in the sunlight that filtered between the leaves.

"The witch?" I asked, curious but intrigued.

"Because you're the best actor at camp this summer, boy or girl," John quickly added. "But don't look at it as being a 'female' role. Something more like a sorcerer."

Without missing a beat, I said: "I'm on it!" excited to dig my teeth into the juicy role.

I'm not sure why, but playing a witch wasn't a big issue with me. I was embracing gender fluidity before anyone had words for it. And let's just say, if they gave Tony Awards for summer stock, I would've won one, hands down!

Hampton Playhouse changed the direction of my life again. Literally. Growing up, I dreamed of going to Los Angeles for college, USC or UCLA. My camp counselors told me that if I was really serious about acting, I had to study in New York. It got me rethinking my post-high school trajectory. But first, I had my plate full being Thespian President and scoring the leads in my senior play and musical.

As "seen" as I felt by Mrs. Bernstein and Mrs. Borts, it was Gail Maudlin, my biology teacher, who really got me. She was one of those teachers who seemed more like a friend. I started hanging out in her back office between classes.

I got the lead role of "Grandpa" in *You Can't Take It With You* and was excited when the faculty picked *Bye Bye Birdie* as our spring musical. I figured they chose that show because the lead role of "Albert" would be a good fit for me. Like Dick Van Dyke, I was an excellent physical comedian, but not a singer. And they knew that my close friend Adrienne would probably get the part of "Rosie" opposite me. We were certain to light up the stage together.

She got the part. I did not.

Adrienne and I also applied to be co-student choreographers. I remember Miss Maudlin called me at home—this was becoming a pattern.

Miss Maudlin: "Stan, how would you like to be the sole student choreographer?"

Me: "But I have no formal dance training." I couldn't tell her my only real experience were those full-out *West Side Story* numbers I did in my bedroom.

"Trust yourself and don't worry about stereotyping roles," Miss Maudlin advised. "And just think, you'd be the first male student choreographer in Southfield High history."

I accepted, as she probably knew I would. And leaped into my new job with gusto. I became a mini-Bob Fosse, creating beautiful stage moments as well as fun, inventive movements. It made me really love dance and want to actually study it.

Also, during my senior year, I had to decide where I was going to go to college. I applied to two places, the University of Michigan and New York University. Applying to U of M was a family tradition. Because my parents and all my aunts and uncles and my brother had gone there, I was expected to go as well. They did have a great theater program, but my heart was set on NYU.

That presented some major hurdles. I had to talk my father into it. He kept insisting I could get the same education in Ann Arbor that I could in New York, causing quite a rift between us. Also, we couldn't afford NYU. Mom called me into her bedroom.

"Is this *really* what you want to do with your life?" she asked. "If it is, I will somehow find the money for you to go. Think about it."

I left her room and went to my bedroom to think over this life-shaping decision. About five minutes later, I was back in her doorway. She looked up from her needlepoint.

"I want to do it!" I proudly proclaimed. She smiled big.

But another major hurdle loomed. I'd have to audition to get in. I found an appropriate monologue, one from William Inge's play, *Dark at the Top of the Stairs*. Mrs. Borts offered to work on it with me, but I declined and rehearsed it on my own.

Two months later, I boarded a plane to New York with my father, who had decided to keep a watchful eye on me, doing everything in his power to discourage my decision.

When I got to NYU on the big day, I had to audition in front of all the other students! Everyone seemed to not "perform" their words but simply said them naturally.

What?! Where was all their carefully choreographed blocking?

I made a last-minute decision and scrapped everything I'd rehearsed, all my elaborate movements and hand gestures. I pulled up a chair and spoke my part directly to the man running the auditions, my stomach doing the Watusi.

"Do you ever get a sick feeling in the pit of your stomach?" I began.

Really. Those were the lines, and that's exactly how I was feeling. At the time, I didn't realize I was "method acting."

A few months later, I got home from school one day to find a letter from NYU in our mailbox. My stomach dropped. Wasn't a big packet an indication you were accepted? This was the thinnest envelope I had ever seen. Like rice paper.

I sat on the couch in my living room staring at the envelope, all alone except for our little dog Toto (yes, like in the movie). I opened the letter, thinking of ways I could avoid going back to school for the rest of my senior year. Fake an illness? Is total humiliation a disease?

But then I read the first few words: *We are happy to say that you've been accepted to NYU/Circle in the Square with a work/study scholarship.*

I screamed at the top of my lungs and jumped in the air. Toto barked wildly. Even she was happy for me.

When I shared the news with people at school the next day, they were thrilled too. Except my drama teacher, Mrs. Borts. I could tell she was hurt that I hadn't sought her coaching or mentioned when I was going to Manhattan to audition. I don't think she ever got over feeling like I knew better than her. To be honest, I think I did. But I still wanted her to be proud of me.

NEXT STOP, GREENWICH VILLAGE

Arriving for college in Manhattan at the tender age of seventeen-and-a-half was frightening. I was so nervous when my mother finished unpacking my stuff and left me on my own in my tiny cinder block dorm room at Weinstein Hall in "The Village." I didn't know any other students. My closest lifelines were my cousins, Ruth and Don Epstein, who lived in New Rochelle. Thank God, they were there for weekend getaways and a home-cooked meal. And a pair of familiar, friendly faces.

But I wasn't alone for long. On my first day at NYU, I met Rande Leaman from Oceanside, Long Island. Our first encounter was when she chased me around the dance floor with a broom in the basement of the shabby Martinique Hotel in midtown Manhattan during a group improv exercise. That, and the fact that she knew and loved *Next Stop, Greenwich Village* as much as I did, clinched the deal. She even looked like Ellen Greene in the movie and dressed in supercool vintage clothing. An interesting mix of items from the 1940s to the 1960s. I'd never met anyone like her and immediately started peppering her with questions.

"Where do you get clothes like that?" "What was it like growing up so close to the city?" "How many Broadway shows have you seen?" "Who the hell are you?!"

So many questions that she got me a Curious George stuffed

animal for my eighteenth birthday. That's always been my nature. Curious about people and the world and wanting to figure out both. Thanks, Cranbrook!

Rande and I got close very quickly. But not in the way she (or my mother) wanted. As much as I tried to be straight, it wasn't in the cards. Rande could've walked away. But she didn't. She was the first person to accept me for who I was and who I loved—even before I could admit it to myself. And her family always made me feel like I was the son (and brother) they never had.

I had other influential young women in my life at NYU besides Rande—Anna Louizos, Diane George, Roberta Zimmerman, and many more. None of them, especially Rande, approved of my first boyfriend, James Mellon Curley. He was an acting student a grade above us at Circle in the Square. And socially, light years from my humble Midwestern upbringing.

Mellon was the "Mellon" of Carnegie Mellon University. His family had a huge home on Park Avenue and owned an island. Why he liked me, with my fake down jacket, big mop of hair, and pencil-thin body, I'll never know. But he did.

While most college students went to coffee shops or movies on their dates, James took me to Studio 54 at the height of its popularity and notoriety. I'd heard of the much talked about, exclusive nightclub that was taking over the city.

When I was with James, we'd be whisked in, past the Bridge and Tunnel crowd, beyond the red velvet ropes, and into this dazzling, old theater. The orchestra seats had been removed, the space turned into a huge dance floor with large cushion areas everywhere, and a big moon that lowered in back with a lighted up cocaine spoon.

All I kept thinking was, "What the hell am I doing here?!" I knew I would never have gotten in if it weren't for James. He reeked of old school money. He also reeked of 70s cologne and booze. James had a drinking problem. I barely knew what that meant back then. But I did know I would be responsible for getting him into a cab at the end of the night and safely back to his East Village apartment.

I can still smell him. And picture his toothy, handsome grin. We were SO different. He lived life on the edge. I always played it safe. He came from A LOT of money. We were hopelessly middle class.

One night at Studio (that's what the kids called it), when James was probably off talking to Halston or Liza, I was sitting on some couches on the dance floor, slightly stoned on pot and nursing a cocktail. This girl sitting nearby started miming someone taking pictures. I thought maybe I was just really wasted. But then she pointed behind me.

I turned around.

There was Andy Warhol, snapping pictures of me. Now, here's the crazy part. I yelled to him over the pulsating disco music, "Stop taking my picture!"

Yeah, I know. I said that to Andy Warhol! Even he looked surprised but stopped and walked away. What was I thinking? I'll tell you. I thought he was taking part of my soul with every picture. I was that kind of stoned. So somewhere in the bowels of the Andy Warhol Museum are pictures of a glassy-eyed Jew, with hair too big and a protruding Adam's apple, in a polyester shirt, looking like he didn't belong.

But I did a lot more during my college years than disco dancing. I got to study with some incredible teachers, most of them women. For acting, I had the formidable and brutally honest Terry Hayden. I liked her tough love approach. I didn't have time to waste with niceties. I had a career to start building.

Terry would often ask, "What are you doing? You're not in the moment. You're walking through it. Why are you avoiding real feelings?"

One day she brought our class to sit in the balcony of the famed Actors Studio to witness the great Lee Strasberg teach. I sat there, imagining artists like Marlon Brando and Marilyn Monroe working in that very space, and realized in that moment that I would never have experienced this at the University of Michigan. Take that, Dad! Bitter, party of one.

I was also excelling at dance classes with my modern dance teacher,

me, bustling away. And somehow, every night, I just happened to land right behind Mr. Nureyev for the curtain call. When the audience jumped to their feet and erupted in screams of "Bravo!" I shut my eyes and pretended those calls of appreciation were meant for me.

My mother wanted to fly in for the show, but I didn't want her to spend the money. I knew she was sacrificing so much to get me to NYU. It's one of my few regrets. I wish she could've shared in that glorious, four-week engagement. I relished every minute of it. Riding on the subway up to 50th Street with my dance bag proudly slung over my shoulder, holding the railing, standing stoically in second position. It was fun to come out of the stage door every night to adoring fans. I knew they weren't there for me, but I believed someday they would be.

During my time home in Michigan that summer, I noticed a book by Gail Parent on my sister's nightstand, *Sheila Levine is Dead and Living in New York*. I started reading it and immediately thought it would make a great play.

When I got back to NYU, I began adapting the book, figured out Gail's agent at CAA, and gave his assistant the number of the front desk at my dorm in case he wanted to contact me. He never did.

I took that as a "yes" that we could perform my adaptation of her best-selling book at school in a workshop production with my class-mates. I know; not exactly kosher. I asked my fellow Circle in the Square student, Michael Engler, to direct it. He's now a big TV and film director, including the *Downton Abbey* movie and *The Gilded Age*. I take total credit for all his success. Naturally, I had Rande star as "Sheila." It was a smash and my first real play.

But I didn't think of myself as a writer. I had simply adapted a book. I still wanted to be an actor. So, when someone came to class one day with an ad from the newspaper about an open call for teen actors/dancers/singers, we all jumped at the chance. It was for a new musical film called *Hot Lunch*, later changed to *Fame*. You might have heard of it.

A bunch of my classmates decided we had to skip school and go wait in line to audition. We didn't care how long it would take; this could be our big break and ticket to stardom. It seemed like anyone from the ages of eight to eighty-eight were there.

I finally made it inside, and a young woman behind a desk took my picture and résumé. I guess she liked what she saw because she handed me a piece of paper with "Montgomery's" monologue on it. I was told to work on it and wait in another line. My friends were all sent home. I think they kept me because I looked like I was still fifteen, the character's age.

A few minutes later, I got called into a room, and suddenly I was being introduced to an older British man, the director, Alan Parker. They filmed me reading my lines. He gave me a few acting notes. I adjusted my performance, and then suddenly I was back outside on the street.

My first major audition, and I got to read for the director. But that's where it ended. I never heard from them. Well, actually, I did *hear* them. As if it to haunt me, *Fame* ended up shooting across the street from my new East Village apartment. At PS 101 on East 9th Street. I had to hear that damn music all summer long!

During my sophomore year, I had a major decision to make. Thanks to Amy Niles, a friend at NYU, I got offered a job as assistant to acclaimed director, Franco Zeffirelli. He was staging *Filamina*, a new play starring his wife, famed actress Joan Plowright. I would have to quit school and head straight to Boston, where the show was having out-of-town tryouts.

I agonized over what to do. My mom never pressured me but patiently suggested we think of all the "pros and cons," her method for solving problems. Eventually, I decided it was more important to stay and finish college. I'm glad I did. The play quickly flopped on Broadway. But I heard his assistant moved to Italy to work with Zeffirelli for many years. *The Golden Girls* would never have been in my life if I'd chosen that path. Although I'm sure I would've met many Sophia Petrillos over there.

While all this was going on, I met someone who would alter my life forever. This was with Jim Berg. We met through a mutual friend, Jack Eckstein, a Parsons Art School student. Parsons was sharing our NYU dorm, and Rande and I fell in with the creative and extremely liberated group of students.

Jim was studying journalism at NYU's University Without Walls. We made each other laugh whenever we'd run into each other on the street. I told him I wished I could write, but I barely read books growing up. We both had similar middle-class, Jewish, suburban upbringings, although his parents had quite a bit more money than mine. And he was way more advanced than me (sexually, spiritually) and a couple years older. He had recently left dorm life and moved into a cute, one-bedroom apartment on University Place and 12th Street, right next door to Cinema Village, a revival movie house. He invited me to see a film there one afternoon, and after, we went up to his apartment to smoke a joint. Somehow, we got on the subject of our love for TV and decided to write a sitcom pilot together. When I found out Jim was also obsessed with *Next Stop, Greenwich Village*, we decided to "adapt" it to a sitcom. Pay homage.

Okay, rip it off.

We called it *Good for One Fare*, a slogan they had on subway tokens back then. We learned TV structure by watching sitcoms on my tiny, black & white set. I'd write down how many scenes they'd have in each half hour episode.

AUGUST 21, 1980   JOURNAL ENTRY

Jim is terrific! I feel so natural and at peace around him. I've never been so in tune with someone else. Our humors really connect! We work so hard, even on weekends. *I hope all this time and commitment will pay off for us one day.*

From the beginning, Jim and I took our careers seriously, and we knew we'd be successful. We weren't necessarily after money, but what money could bring: freedom. Freedom to create what was truly in our hearts and minds. I don't know why we were so confident at that young age, probably because we were both raised with the idea that we could do anything.

Early on, we came up with this agreement—Jim would get his name first in the credits, but our company name would be Zimmerman/ Berg. Another thing we decided was to not talk during weekends. That way, when we got to work on Monday, it would be fresh and exciting.

During my last year of college, Amy Niles came through with another intriguing offer. She was now working at TNI Casting and wanted me to audition for the part of a young Washington DC page on a new ensemble sitcom pilot for CBS. I came in and read for her boss, Julie Hughes. I was so nervous, my face was shaking. I guess I wasn't a total embarrassment because I got a callback. The pilot wasn't picked up, but it did lead to an internship at Theatre Now, a theater management company connected with TNI. They handled almost all the big Broadway shows, which is why I got comps to practically every show that year.

At Theatre Now, I met Leonard Finger, who was producing a new Mark Connelly play called *A Stitch in Time* for Broadway. We got to talking, and my next semester, I moved over to his office across the street at 1501 Broadway. Unfortunately, Mark died before Opening Night, and all his old lady investors pulled their money from the show.

Leonard ended up getting a few more small gigs, and I'd go to plays to scout actors for him. I got to witness the dynamic Jenifer Lewis in her New York debut in *El Bravo*, a new, Off-Broadway musical. The minute she walked on stage, I knew she was going to be a star.

I also saw the seedy side of the business—the casting couch. Cute, young actors would be traded between male agents and casting directors. I was disheartened that this was the way things worked. Not based on talent.

One of the actors that came through our office was an adorable Midwestern boy with a military haircut since he had just finished filming his first movie, *Taps*. Tom Cruise. He was so excited about this gig, working with such actors as Sean Penn, Timothy Hutton, and George C. Scott, that he was literally jumping up and down on our office sofa. Years later, I wasn't surprised to see him do the same on *The Oprah Winfrey Show*.

As much as I didn't like to see the way these boys were treated like fresh meat, I did learn an extremely valuable lesson from Leonard. One day, he needed to get a script to Elaine Stritch's apartment, and I had to find her address.

"But how?" I asked. We didn't have computers or IMDB Pro to look up her representation.

"You'll figure it out," he replied, swooping out the door to dine with an older, rich female investor at Joe Allen's.

I was freaked out. I didn't know what to do, so I sat down and started to make a list of all the people I knew in show business, even if they were somebody's assistant, or dog walker, or second cousin twice removed. I began frantically calling them and asking if they knew anyone who might have some connection to Elaine Stritch. I pulled in every favor I could.

By the time Leonard returned from lunch, I had the address. It's a method I use to this day. If there's something I want, I sit and figure out how to get it. I don't stop until I do. If I hit a roadblock, I work around it. Like a maze. This process has served me well.

While all this was going on, Jim and I were still writing TV half-hour comedy pilots on spec. Using his copy of the *Writers Market*, we found a young agent, Seth Kadish, who worked at an agency that handled mostly sports and news talent. He was looking to add some young writer clients to his roster. He sent one of our pilot scripts out to LA. It got interest from Gary Keeper, a comedy development executive at Paramount TV. Gary asked Seth what else we had written.

Obviously, Seth couldn't say, "Term papers."

Here's where fate seemed to play a part. In high school, Gary was good friends with my boss, Leonard Finger. And I had handed Leonard a message from Gary two days prior, not knowing that our paths would cross this way. What are the odds?! Leonard offered to call Gary and put in a good word for us.

A few weeks later, Jim's parents said they'd pay for him to join them in California for a cousin's bar mitzvah. We decided I should go out there at the same time so we could meet Gary and hopefully make a few more industry contacts. I called my childhood best friend, now living in Woodland Hills, and asked if he wanted a visitor. He was thrilled, and Jim and I started planning our first business trip.

I'd been to LA once before. For our thirteenth birthdays, my parents offered me and my siblings our own trip with them. Anywhere in the world. My brother chose Israel. Guess where I picked? Hollywood, naturally. I loved every second of it. We even got to meet movie stars. Well, one star. While leaving the Brown Derby after a fabulous lunch, a large pepper mill fell off the table and onto the floor in front of us. My mother picked it up and handed it back to an older woman with jet black hair, tightly pulled back.

As soon as we stepped out of the restaurant, my father asked, "Do you know who that was?"

I shook my head, "No."

He said, "Ann Miller!"

I desperately wanted to rush back in. But what would I have said to her? "Can you make some calls to the studio for a nice Jewish boy who's dying to be an actor? I can give you some pens I got for my bar mitzvah." I chickened out. My one chance to get discovered. So close. This trip with Jim, I wasn't about to let that chance slip by again.

I had been to a Hollywood studio on that previous trip. But touring the Universal backlot on a tram with other tourists isn't the same as driving up to the famous arches on the Paramount lot and the guard handing us a pass with our names on it. We parked our cheap rental car and followed the studio map to Gary Keeper's office.

AUGUST 28, 1981   JOURNAL ENTRY

Jim and I had a marvelous time with Gary
Keeper. We ate at the commissary and then
walked around the lot. On the inside, I was
like a little kid in a candy store, but on the
outside, we kept it very cool. I can't believe
how beautiful it is here. The palm trees are
something else. It will be so depressing to
return to my tiny fifth floor walk-up studio
apartment on 15th St. I could really get into
living out here. Actually, I don't think it's
that far off.

Gary had two pieces of advice: Move to LA since that's where all the TV action was. And write a spec script for a sitcom that's already on the air. That way, producers in Hollywood could see if we could recreate the sound of existing characters. Jim and I didn't waste a second and began a script for *Alice*, the hit CBS sitcom starring Linda Lavin.

At the same time, my job with Leonard Finger wasn't working out. He wasn't finding casting jobs, so he couldn't afford to pay my paltry salary. I was sick of being poor in New York and started to seriously think about moving to LA. Jim wasn't ready to go. He was happy since he landed an apartment with exposed brick *and* a boyfriend. But I could sense that things wouldn't be happening for me in the city, and it was getting too expensive to stay there. Extra work on such films as *The Chosen* and Woody Allen's *Zelig* were not going to cover rent and food. I was starting to feel depressed.

DECEMBER 16, 1981   JOURNAL ENTRY

It seems like everybody is having nice things
happen to them. But I'm still looking for my
first big break. I want it so bad. But right
now, I feel ugly, lonely, and sad. I don't

> know how much more I can take. Jim refuses to
> go to California until we sell something, and
> I cannot find a job in NYC. How much lower can
> I sink? I must be pretty close to rock bottom.
> If nothing comes through, I plan on leaving
> this fucking town mid-May.

Nothing else came through. And there was nothing keeping me in New York, except the constant reminder of who I really was and how I looked. At that time, the preppy look was in, and my wild, crazy hair and geeky body were not exactly the height of fashion. It was all Brooke Shields and Gloria Vanderbilt and the beautiful blond boys from Studio 54. I had to get out. So, what did I do? I decided to move to LA. The city of pretty people. What was I thinking?!

Gary Keeper had become our mentor and promised to "turn us on to a lot of business contacts." I called my high school friend again and arranged to rent an extra room in the house he was staying at in Woodland Hills. My brother offered to loan me his car for the summer. I bought a one-way ticket to LA.

MAY 19, 1982   JOURNAL ENTRY

> Well, I'm leaving NY June 2nd! I'll miss it.
> But nothing is happening here for me, except
> Jim! I feel bad because our writing is final-
> ly clicking but no sales yet! We had a pass
> from our *Alice* spec. Sydney Julien, an exec
> at Embassy (Norman Lear's company), wrote an
> encouraging letter and sent us three sample
> TV scripts. I guess we can't be all that bad?

3

CALIFORNIA, HERE I COME!

My *mother met me in San Francisco,* and together we drove my brother's car down the coast. Our last stop was Santa Barbara. I woke up to find my mom had already been out and about, investigating the beautiful city on the glistening Pacific Ocean. She vowed to leave dirty, snowy Detroit and move there. We packed up the car and headed for Hollywood!

My stomach was in knots, like before a performance in a play. I knew I was doing the right thing, but so much was unsettled. I didn't really doubt that I would be successful. It was just a matter of how long it would take. My parents instilled in us that we were bright and could achieve anything we set our minds to. Now I had to get the rest of the world to get on board.

Upon arriving in town, Gary Keeper got me an interview with Lenore French at Paramount for a writer's apprentice program. Already my life seemed to be turning around. I wondered if this could be our big break.

But soon, I grew frustrated. I was in a nice house in the Valley with a pool, but the apprentice job fell through. I'd drag the olive-colored rotary phone with a long extension cord out to the pool, waiting for one of my new contacts to call back. The phone never rang. I was also extremely isolated at this house by myself. My friend and his two room-mates were always at work. At night, we'd head to West Hollywood.

But during the day, I was going stir-crazy all alone. I couldn't relax. I wanted to do something to move our career forward, but there was nothing to do. And I couldn't work without Jim. Sydney Julien recommended we write another spec, so Jim and I agreed that I'd come back to New York for ten days and we'd bang one out.

We decided to write a script for the new NBC comedy, *Love, Sidney,* starring Tony Randall and Swoosie Kurtz. It was a groundbreaking show in which the "Sidney" character was a homosexual, even though it was NEVER referred to in the series. Jim and I worked on the story and structure before my trip, so once I landed in New York, we could hit the ground running. We wrote diligently every day. At night, I'd visit friends. Jim bought us tickets to this new, hit, Off-Broadway play that had recently moved to Broadway—*Torch Song Trilogy.* July 11, 1982, we sat mesmerized by the hysterical and poignant script and the dynamic duo of Harvey Fierstein and Estelle Getty. Little did we know we'd be writing for her one day.

Upon returning to the West Coast, my mood sank again. I missed my East Coast friends, I didn't have a job, and there was no love in my life. This transition to LA was a lot harder than I expected.

After much nagging, Jim agreed to give California a try. I thought it would be easier with us both in the same city to be able to "take" meetings and make contacts. We were good together, and when people were around us, they felt that energy. I knew in my heart we were an unbeatable pair!

Jim planned on coming to LA September 1, and we decided to live together. Securing a place fell on my shoulders. I found this super-cute hillside house in Silver Lake. A two-bedroom with a separate entrance under the main house. It had killer views looking west out to Hollywood and Griffith Observatory. Silver Lake has a kind of funky New York vibe, which I thought Jim would appreciate. But once here, he wasn't happy. He wasn't used to living with anyone. And he missed his boyfriend, Fred.

In the meantime, I needed to get a job to have some cash coming in. My savings were shrinking at an alarming rate. I had returned my brother's car to him, so I needed to find a job within walking distance of our house. Since my work résumé only included The Americana Movie Complex during high school, I applied to the nearby Vista Movie Theater and got a job as an usher/ticket taker. It was a revival house, and my duties would include changing the marquee every night.

My first day on the job, they made me climb this tall, rickety ladder and put up the letters for the next film to be showing—Lina Wertmuller's *Swept Away by An Unusual Destiny in the Blue Sea of August*. I did, but when I came down from the ladder, I said they had to make me assistant manager. I was not getting up there again and risking my life for titles that long. For some reason, they agreed.

In the meantime, I sent my headshots around town for acting jobs and extra work. When I heard about an open call for a little indie comedy called *Risky Business*, I had Jim drive me to the audition on Robertson Boulevard, just south of Melrose. The street was packed with young Hollywood hopefuls.

They must have liked my youthful teenage look, because I received a call time and place to arrive for shooting. It was on Larchmont Boulevard, staged to look like suburban Chicago. I was surprised to find out that my scene would have me and a couple young guys walking down the street with the star of the film, my ol' pal, Tom Cruise. His character, Joel, would run toward us, put his arms around our shoulders, and talk us into coming to his house party. Not just any house party, one with hooker friends of Lana, the character played by Rebecca De Mornay.

Between takes, I got up the nerve and reminded Tom that we met before in Leonard Finger's office in New York. I left out the part about him bouncing on our sofa. He said he remembered. Or maybe he was merely being polite.

We did a bunch of takes, and then when I was signing my time-card, a production assistant came up and pulled me aside. "Hey, we were wondering if you're available to do another day of work for us."

"Sure!" I quickly jumped in. I was flattered.

"Well, I do have to tell you, it will be a night shoot at the hooker party. And some nudity may be required."

Here's where my active imagination went into overdrive. I somehow conjured up in my crazy, little head that Tom requested me specifically. Maybe to get a little personal time with me, if you know what I mean. (C'mon, we've all heard the rumors.) But because of my continued body issues, I said *no*. The production assistant seemed disappointed but understood. Upon seeing the movie when it came out, I noticed there was no nudity in that scene. Not only did I miss out on some much-needed cash, but today I might've been Mrs. Tom Cruise!

On the writing front, through Gary Keeper, Jim and I were able to get our scripts read by quite a few agents. We were met with A LOT of rejection letters. I saved them all.

"I'm just not sufficiently enthusiastic to consider representation at this time."—Todd Bergesen, Robinson-Weintraub & Associates

"Due to the size of our office and the resultant time restraints, we're unable to take on your representation at this time."—Martin A. Hurwitz, Ziegler/Diskant, Inc.

"Though the consensus of opinion is that your writing is good and shows potential, we're focusing at this time on more established writers."—Ellen Glick, ICM

"Hang in there. You're talented and I'm sure you'll do very well."—Mark Rosen, CAA

"We feel that you have a lot of talent that will eventually come together."—Gregg-Edward Moscoe/Jim Preminger Agency

Jim and I finally signed with Mark Harris, an agent at the Artists Group. He suggested we write another spec. We had three under our belt. All generally liked by people in the business. But as Gary Keeper pointed out, "Every executive has a pile of scripts on their desk. Yours can't just be good; it has to REALLY stand out!"

So, we agreed to write another one. We just didn't know which show. Then Gary invited us to a taping of a new NBC sitcom at

Paramount. That was all we could afford for entertainment.

During the first break between scenes, Jim and I turned to each other, bursting with episode ideas. That show was *Cheers*. We felt *Cheers* was the perfect combination for us—smart characters and witty dialogue. Since the show wasn't on the air yet, the market wasn't flooded with spec scripts from it. And no one knew the massive hit it would eventually become.

The minute we finished our spec script, things started to happen for us. Suddenly we were getting called in for meetings. Our first was for a new ABC sitcom that Gary had been involved with, *Just Our Luck*, about a hapless LA TV weatherman who finds a bottle on the Venice boardwalk and out pops a Black, hip genie.

You heard right.

Gary had left Paramount and was now working at Lorimar with Chuck and Larry Gordon, who rose to fame on the Eddie Murphy movie, *48 Hours*. Back then, you came in early for your meeting and watched the pilot, then met with the creators/executive producers. Waiting in the lobby, we heard the writing team in the interview before us. Everyone was cracking up. Jim and I panicked.

Jim said, "What were we supposed to do, prepare jokes?"

We had none. We weren't stand-up comedians.

Using what I learned during my NYU audition, I said, "We're charming, funny guys. Let's just be ourselves."

Suddenly, the office door opened and we were whisked inside.

MAY 26, 1983   JOURNAL ENTRY

We just got back from our first meeting for
a TV show job. I think they're going to offer
us a staff job, or at least a script assignment. They made such a to-do about how young
we were. I'm not crazy about the show, but we
need to get started somewhere . . . No sooner
do I put down the pen—that something FINALLY

> happens! I cannot, I repeat, cannot believe
> it. *Just Our Luck* called our agent to make an
> offer for us for staff positions. He also got
> a call from ABC, who is hot for us for the
> new Madeline Kahn series. Now what?! I'm too
> excited to write.

Oh Madeline was a new sitcom starring the comic genius Madeline Kahn. I LOVED her in *Paper Moon*, *What's Up Doc?*, just about everything. We struggled with what to do, but ultimately, we felt an allegiance to our mentor Gary and accepted the *Just Our Luck* offer.

We had to report to the MGM lot in Culver City on Monday morning. So, on Friday afternoon, I turned my work keys into the Vista and we impulsively drove to LAX to spend the weekend in New York. With no plane tickets. Jim had a credit card. I had my mom's.

On the way to the airport, I remember rolling down the window and yelling out at the top of my lungs, "THIS IS LIFE!" And it was. We purchased tickets on the spot to New York. One last hurrah in the city we loved before embarking on a new chapter of our professional lives.

That first day at work back in LA, we were so nervous, we stopped in every bathroom on the lot from the parking structure to our office. We were anxious to get to the Clark Gable Building before the other writers. We couldn't believe it when they showed us to our own office. It had two big desks facing each other. And two phones! We immediately sat in our large swivel chairs and put our feet up on the desks. We had arrived.

And so had the other writers.

They took one look at us and were instantly put off. First, we looked super young. And second, we were practically bouncing off the walls with so much pep and energy. Not tainted yet by the bitterness of Hollywood.

The executive producers, Rick Kellard and Bob Comfort, called everyone to the conference room for our first meeting. Jim and I thought that as staff writers we'd just be getting everybody coffee. Oh, no. We were sitting at the table with everyone else. They expected us to come back from lunch and pitch out a complete episode.

What?! We've never done that before.

Everyone left for lunch off the lot. We went to D. B. Coopers, a nearby restaurant on Overland Avenue in Culver City. I don't think either of us ate much. Our stomachs were in knots again. We somehow figured out a story and headed back to the studio. Luckily, we didn't have to pitch first, so we watched how everyone else did it. At the time, there were no classes in sitcom writing. We learned by doing. And watching. They liked what we pitched and sent us off to write the outline. Not everyone was so fortunate. Some writers had to go back to the drawing board. That night we brought champagne to our agents to celebrate.

We seemed to shine on *Just Our Luck*. The other writers soon warmed up to us, and our office became party central. We bonded with Ria Nepas, the female writer next door to us. She became like our "Sally," the Rose Marie character from *The Dick Van Dyke Show*. We socialized a lot with her outside of work.

Kellard & Comfort liked our first draft, and it became the first one filmed. And we had two special guest stars—Roy Orbison and Don Cornelius. I could kick myself for not taking Don up on his offer to go to a taping of his classic dance program, *Soul Train*. I LOVED that show growing up.

We were immediately given a second episode to write. But then things took a turn. Word got out what *Just Our Luck* was about, and the NAACP filed a complaint. They didn't say our names, but it mentioned that the producers hired two (White) inexperienced writers over anyone of color. Especially since one of the leads was Black. And they didn't approve of the Black genie referring to the White main character as "Master." That may have worked on *I Dream of Jeanie*, but not anymore. I mean, I don't blame them, but I can't believe no one at the studio or network was sensitive to that issue until right before it aired in September. It was wisely edited out.

The producers scrambled and hired another writing team, one Black, one White. The pilot episode airdate on ABC was around the corner. The studio planned a big premiere party at Chasen's, a fancy restaurant in Beverly Hills. Our reps urged us to bring a "beard" to the event. Beards were straight women that gay men brought to functions so they would appear straight. The woman had to be in on the ruse.

I decided to bring my new friend, film actress Diane Franklin. I met her through my friend Rande, who was now married, so her beard card was revoked. Diane seemed like the perfect "plus one" since she was starting to make a name for herself in Hollywood as the beautiful, young ingenue in such films as *The Last American Virgin* and *Amityville II*. I thought she could also make some good contacts for herself at the party.

The minute we arrived, we were surrounded by all these lecherous male executives and agents. Married or not, they all wanted to know the nature of our relationship because they all wanted to have sex with Diane. My little charade had failed.

From a business perspective, people in the industry were starting to take notice of Zimmerman/Berg. Suddenly, we were the "Flavor of the Month." A few months earlier, we couldn't get agents to return our calls; now they all wanted to wine and dine us to sign with them. Some even offered to get us into one of Hugh Hefner's Playboy Mansion parties. Being in the closet, we couldn't tell them that wasn't going to sway us in the least.

After a while, all those free lunches became a chore. Especially if they were with some boring, suited, straight guys. The female agent meals were always more fun.

Bob O'Connor, head of comedy development at CBS, read our *Cheers* spec, heard great things about us, and wanted us to do a pilot at his network. This was unheard of in those days for inexperienced staff writers. Usually, you had to be on multiple shows for years to get a blind script commitment. Even Gary Keeper said it was too soon in our career to do one. But Bob was insistent, and our agent told Gary that if he wasn't interested, we'd make the deal with another producer at Lorimar.

Minutes later, Gary was on board and suggested we meet the next morning to discuss ideas at Junior's Deli in Westwood. I wanted to go someplace where we could be seen. I'm no dummy. The Bel-Air Hotel it was. On the way to our table, Gary introduced us around the dining room. And he liked a lot of our ideas too. We settled on one and began to develop it with him.

I couldn't believe how fast our lives had turned around in less than a year in LA. I could now afford my own car and bought a light blue Toyota Corolla. I also found my own place to rent. It was the side of a house on Treasure Trail in the Hollywood Hills off of Cahuenga Boulevard. Small, but super-cute.

Our very first network pitch would be at CBS Television City, the home of none other than *The Carol Burnett Show*. We sat at the end of a long, wood table and pitched our little hearts out, reading directly from colored index cards. When we finished, we looked up to Bob O'Connor.

He took a beat, then said to us, "Is there anything else you want to do?"

My heart sank. "You mean as a career?" I asked. People in the room laughed.

Bob clarified, "I meant another series idea."

"Ohhhh." I breathed a sigh of relief.

We wrote a really funny script, kind of a female *Odd Couple*, called *Late Bloomers*. And we got to use our mothers' first names (Faye and Susanne) for the two leading roles. Everyone really liked the script— our producers (The Gordon brothers), the studio (Lorimar), and the network. We started talking casting.

Two actors at the top of everyone's wish list were Louise Lasser (*Mary Hartman, Mary Hartman*) and Bea Arthur (*Maude*). We thought

Bea was too old for the role and kept pushing for Marlo Thomas (*That Girl*). But then at the last minute, the network president found an old script about two divorced women with kids who move in together, called *Kate & Allie*. Our pilot died a quick death. As did *Just Our Luck*. ABC canceled it before airing all the episodes we shot, and we had to pack up our offices.

I wasn't too upset. I liked our coworkers and knew we'd keep in touch. But I loved having money coming in. With that, I could explore LA, especially downtown, before it was hip. The city back then was buzzing with creative energy. And now I could afford to take my friends out for fancy dinners at cool restaurants, like Muse on Melrose. I was also hanging out in West Hollywood more and having little romances here and there. But nothing serious.

Although we were out of a job, I refused to go back to work at the Vista. Our new agent, Jack Dytman, started getting us pitch meetings for episodes of existing shows. And we landed a few. Z&B, which Jack was calling us now, were back in the game!

First up was *Brothers*, a Showtime series and one of the first featuring a gay lead. We pitched them a bunch of episode ideas, but they decided that we should adapt our *Cheers* spec for this show. Working with the producers on that show was my first experience with cocaine in Hollywood. Although at the time, I had no idea what was going on. It wasn't until years later that Jim pointed out that when one of the producers left to go to the bathroom, he came back totally wired, buzzing with ideas. And a little white powder on the end of his nose. I was so naïve. Went right over my head.

Then we wrote an episode for *Spencer*, starring Chad Lowe, until he abruptly quit the day we handed in our script. They recast the lead, changed the name to *Under One Roof*, and refocused the show on his parents, played by Ronny Cox and Mimi Kennedy.

Probably the biggest episode we worked on was for a syndicated version of the hit movie, *Fame*. Yes, it was haunting me again. This time in a good way, as a writer. We met with the producers of the series and pitched them a bunch of ideas. They bought one about a student who gets a bad review in the school paper.

And guess who ended up playing that student? None other than Janet Jackson.

The episode was directed by the great Debbie Allen. She used the title track from Janet's first album, "Dream Street," and put it into the show as a musical/dance number. Debbie filmed this beautiful story about a young actress coming to Hollywood in the 40s. It started in faded brown sepia tone, then burst into color for a spectacular MGM ending. I was never so proud as when it played on the huge video screens at Revolver, a popular gay bar on Santa Monica Blvd in West Hollywood.

Jim and I got asked to pitch for the newish NBC series, *Valerie*, starring Valerie Harper (Rhoda from *The Mary Tyler Moore Show*). The day we went in, Valerie left the show in a very publicized and nasty departure. We must be a jinx.

The producers ultimately brought in Sandy Duncan and renamed the show *The Hogan Family*. We landed the gig, but things got complicated when we got asked to pitch for another NBC series. This was for a brand-new show that wasn't even on the air yet. It was a female ensemble comedy about four older women living together in Miami. Can you guess? It was called *The Golden Girls*.

THE GOLDEN GIRLS

nother Top Five question I hear is, "How did you get the job
on *The Golden Girls?*"

Our agent got us a meeting to pitch for an open writing assignment.
Which means if they like one of your pitches, you're hired to write one
episode. Nothing more. We went to Sunset Gower Studios to watch a
tape of the pilot. That's where they were going to start filming the series
at the end of the summer. Our minds began to swirl with ideas. Here's
a never-before-seen list of what we were planning to pitch:

Dorothy meets a man that everyone dislikes. Act Break—Dorothy
moves in with him.

Dorothy retires from teaching.

Mildred dies, Sophia has a change of life and suddenly becomes
sweet.

One of the girls has a car accident and becomes afraid to get back
behind the wheel.

They find a homeless man in the lanai—"Down & Out in Miami."

Blanche becomes a "sugar mama" to a 30ish artist (he moves in?).
He's a bad painter.

Rose joins an EST-type group after meeting one of the cult leaders.

Like *Harold & Maude*, a 19-year-old guy becomes infatuated with
Sophia.

When we returned to Sunset Gower a few weeks later, we found out that we not only had to pitch to Kathy Speer and Terry Grossman, the married writer/executive producers, but also to the two main non-writing producers, Tony Thomas and Paul Witt. Witt/Thomas were huge at the time, having produced such hits as *Soap*, *Benson*, and *It's a Living*, among others.

Kathy and Terry seemed nice, but we were extremely intimidated by Paul and Tony. They were strong, gruff men who probably got ahead by not taking crap from anyone. That was the style of doing business back then.

Our pitches did not go over well. They weren't buying any. When the last one was rejected, we thanked them for taking the time, got up, and started to leave. Literally in the door jam, something came over me—I'm not sure what. I turned back to them and shouted, "What if Rose's mother came to visit?"

I think they were a little surprised by my outburst. After what seemed like a long pause but was probably only a few seconds, Kathy said, "And . . .?"

Jim and I started riffing.

Jim: "What if Rose's mother came to visit?"

Then I finished his sentence, like we had begun to do, with: "And Rose treats her like a little girl." An issue I was familiar with from my mother's experience with my grandmother.

They looked at each other; then Paul said, "Come back in and sit down."

We did, and we all started brainstorming on the spot.

We came up with the episode known as "Rose's Mother." During that meeting, we also worked on a B-story, the secondary story. Every sitcom episode has an A-storyline (the main story) and a B one. Ours for this one was about Blanche going out with her handsome, much younger trainer. That's why this episode is also known as "Blanche & the Younger Man."

Satisfied with the structure, we were sent off to write a detailed outline.

I don't think Jim and I exhaled until we were safely in our car in the studio parking structure. Then we let out loud screams of joy. Luckily, there were no security guards nearby, or we would've been escorted off the premises.

With that cast and the Witt/Thomas pedigree, we knew this was a big shot for us. So, we had to put all our energy and focus into it. After much deliberation, we decided to pass on writing that freelance episode for *The Hogan Family*.

We attended a couple of the first live studio tapings to get a sense of where the episodes and characters were going. We were nervous wrecks when we handed in our first draft. You never know how people will react. Especially because the writer/producers on staff know the characters much better than outside writers ever could. To our surprise, we got very few notes. Many of our lines stayed in from the first rough draft to the shooting script, a rarity on any show. Some of our original lines have now become classics, like:

Dorothy: "The only time I get in that position is when I give birth."
Dorothy: "In what, Blanche, dog years?"
Rose: "Stopping me from living isn't going to stop me from dying."

That last one, I'm particularly proud of. When I'm asked my favorite line we ever wrote for the series, I usually say that one.

Now, it's extremely hard to get a first draft right, especially for such novice writers as us. The producers were so impressed they asked us to come on as staff writers. We should've had a bump up in title from our last show to "story editors," which would have meant on-screen credit for every episode, but Witt/Thomas wouldn't budge in the negotiations. They knew this was the most coveted job in town, and they had the upper hand. We accepted and instantly got a parking spot and office at Sunset Gower. Since they were already in the midst of the first half of the season, there would be no time for a learning curve. We were thrown into the deep end of the pool.

In the beginning, we were often sent off to come up with joke options for the end of scenes, otherwise known as "buttons." Sitting in our office, watching us like a play, was Chris Lloyd (later the co-creator and executive producer of *Modern Family*). He was a young guy whose father, the legendary sitcom writer, David Lloyd (*The Mary Tyler Moore Show, Taxi*, etc.), was friends with Paul and Tony. Also working there, but as a PA (production assistant), was Dan Palladino. I remember seeing this cute guy with really great hair walking the halls and having a crush on him.

But most of the time, Jim and I were in a perpetual state of fear, especially writing these buttons. We didn't consider ourselves "joke" writers. This would be our schooling, like Comedy Writing 101. We had to come up with four to six jokes for each area that needed work, then go back in the room and pitch them to the writer/producers. No pressure there. We saved ourselves a lot of time when we realized Bea Arthur didn't need words. Just by staring daggers at Rose or Blanche, she could get a huge laugh. I don't know any other actor who can do that.

Now it's called "side-eye" or "throwing shade." At the time, we wrote it as "Dorothy shoots her a look." Not sure if we made up that term, but we still use it today. We also learned a few other tricks. We discovered that Rue/Blanche sounded funniest, and more Southern, when we gave her words that ended in "r" or "er" or names like "Dirk." If you listen closely to our scripts, they're filled with words like: "mother," "lover," "Betty Crocker."

The Golden Girls was a multi-cam show, meaning scenes were filmed with multiple cameras. We were told that concept was created by Desi Arnaz for *I Love Lucy*. Truth is, it was used a few years earlier on shows like *Amos 'n Andy*. What Desilu Studios brought to the format was using 35mm film instead of 16mm and filming with a multiple-camera setup before a live studio audience.

Our schedule on tape weeks went like this: Monday morning the cast and crew would meet in a big rehearsal hall for the "table read." It would be the first chance everyone would get to hear the script that would be shot at the end of the week. At the table read, the director of each episode read the stage directions and the writers' names before the actors begin going through the script. We shyly looked up and smiled at the mention of our names, but otherwise kept a low profile. As newbies, we didn't know the lay of the land yet. I'm glad we weren't aware that in the beginning, Bea Arthur was not happy about how young the writers were. I have a feeling she was referring to us since we looked like high school students. But we heard she changed her tune when she saw the quality of the scripts week after week.

After the table read, everyone goes upstairs while the executive producers get notes from the studio and network. The actors rehearse unless there's a major rewrite. In our offices, we'd fix any issues or start work on other episodes.

Tuesday morning, the actors rehearse again. Then in the afternoon, we all go down to the "floor" to watch the "studio run-through." We didn't meet the ladies formally until our first run-through. I remember hearing, "Pssst!" We turned around to see Estelle Getty. She beckoned me and Jim to follow her behind the set. Of course, we did, with some trepidation.

Then she whispered, "I got your backs, since you're one of us." We thought she meant Jewish.

She clarified, "No, gay! But your secret's safe with me." Then she winked at us.

Estelle wasn't gay herself but considered herself an honorary member of "the tribe" since she spent so many years playing Harvey Fierstein's mom in *Torch Song Trilogy*. A friendship was born. But the whole situation made us realize that we were not in a friendly atmosphere, as far as Witt/Thomas were concerned.

I know people find it hard to believe that we had to remain in the closet on such an open and progressively written show. *The Golden Girls* tackled many taboo subjects of the time (and through today): race, AIDS, suicide, ageism, PTSD, addiction, etc. They were done with humor, intelligence, and always honesty. We were told to not make them like a "Very Special Episode" of *The Facts of Life*. The stories had to feel organic to these characters. Maybe that's why the show is still so popular.

That night after the studio run-through, we went back to the writers' room for more rewrites if needed. And more food was ordered in.

Let me explain a writers' room: There's a big, long table where we all sit, eat, laugh, and complain a lot. Writers usually pick "their spot" early in the season. Also at the table is the writers' assistant, the young person who takes down everything the writers say in case we can use it in a script. Back in the day, we didn't have computers, so it was all done longhand. That has to be one of the hardest jobs on a TV show, but it's also one of the most rewarding. Not only do you get to see how a show is constructed, but most move up the ranks to become writers and hopefully run their own shows one day.

The writers' room on *The Golden Girls* was a bit different. Because of the show's high stakes, the executive producers, Paul Witt and Tony Thomas, sat in on rewrites. That's not normal. Usually, non-writing producers give their notes and then go back to their fancy Beverly Hills homes (and their second wives and blended families), leaving the staff to order dinner, then settle in for a long night to deal with all the notes. Right away, Jim and I saw the other writers acting differently when Paul and Tony were in the room. Mind you, *The Golden Girls* creator, Susan Harris, was NEVER in the room. She was suffering from Epstein-Barr, an autoimmune disease that left her very weak. We always enjoyed the weeks that it was a Susan Harris script because we knew there would be few rewrites. With everyone else's scripts, it was open season to change anything that didn't seem to be working. And if those four brilliant actors couldn't make it work, it didn't work.

On a hit show, the studio and network give few notes. If it's not a hit, everything is questioned and picked apart. Luckily with *The Golden Girls*, the actors rarely had notes. And contrary to online gossip, the actors DID NOT AD-LIB. It's good acting that makes it seem so real. Paul and Tony stuck around to make sure every joke was a home run and the scripts and stories were as tight as possible.

We'd only worked in one writers' room before *The Golden Girls*, but something didn't feel quite right. Even as a novice, I knew that a room built on fear did not create an atmosphere that felt free. You have to be able to say the stupidest things because you never know what can spark an idea or joke from another writer. But in this room, Jim and I saw other, more experienced people write down their joke and show it to the person sitting next to them at the table. If that person smiled and nodded, they'd feel comfortable with pitching it out loud. That seems counterproductive. Of course, when Witt/Thomas were not in the room, we all could be our usual, silly selves.

The rest of the week was—Wednesday mornings, actors rehearsing again, then you go down in the afternoon for the network run-through. More rewrites would follow, and more food in Styrofoam containers. Thursdays, cameras came in, and the cast and director would show the crew the blocking. On Fridays, to have more options in editing, we filmed each episode twice in front of a live studio audience, with a meal break in between. We were always afraid one of the ladies, besides Estelle, would sit with us at dinner. We wouldn't know what to say if they started talking to us.

Back then, writers were not on the floor (meaning in the studio); we were all in a trailer in the parking lot, usually with the network executives. The director and AD were in an adjacent trailer. Everyone had folding director chairs with their names embossed on the back. But not me and Jim. We were forced to stand during the entire filming. Was this intentional? It felt as if Witt/Thomas didn't consider us "real writers."

JANUARY 20, 1986   JOURNAL ENTRY

Paul Witt and Tony Thomas are so cold to us.
It's a shame because everybody else seems to
be warming up. Chris Lloyd supposedly has been
negotiating for next year. After the nice

```
response to our script and the fact we've been
asked to do our third script, I feel pretty
confident. If they don't ask us back, it's
their loss. One downside has been I don't
get to spend as much time with Jim outside of
work. He was (or is) my best friend. But after
long hours at work, I know he wants to spend
his time with Fred. I've got to come to grips
with that. It's not easy. I do miss him.
```

Since you spend so many hours together in that room, you end up talking about EVERYTHING. Except for me and Jim. Not only did our agents tell us to keep our homosexuality on the down-low, but we remembered what Estelle told us. So, on Mondays, when everybody was going on about what they did over the weekend, I could never say, "I went dancing at Studio One in West Hollywood." Or "I met this really cute boy at a pool party in the hills." We also learned to hide our true selves when we'd hear people's responses to certain subjects.

I distinctly remember one day in the room saying, "Jim and I went to a garage sale in Silver Lake. I love used clothing and found these really cool, old sweaters."

Since Silver Lake was a known gay enclave, the writers all began chiming in: "You can't wear those sweaters; you could catch AIDS." "That's probably whose clothes they were selling." "You have to burn them the minute you get home!"

This was early in the disease, and we didn't have a lot of information, but it still seemed drastic. They instilled so much anxiety in me that when I got home that night, I immediately threw the sweaters into the garbage can.

So, we continued leading a double life. We were out to our families and friends but not at work. Growing up, I only heard the word "gay" used as a weapon. By now, we were so used to living a lie, it was second nature in order to survive in the world.

We had a more important issue at hand, like keeping our job. We had a one-year contract with an option for a second. At the producers' discretion. And there were so many signs that we weren't fully accepted by Paul and Tony. They never seemed interested in getting to know us as people. I knew their manner was tough, but it didn't make for a hospitable working environment. We even heard a story, probably folklore, that a writer was so pissed off at them, they took a dump on their desk one night after work and left it there for them to discover the next morning. I thought of doing that, but my grandmother would never approve.

We didn't let their attitude stop us. We worked extremely hard and only voiced our concerns to each other.

We learned so much on that show. Especially how to craft a joke, making sure the humor came from the character. We also learned that you NEVER switch a joke from one character's mouth to another. Each must be specific to the individual. Especially if the script has already been read and rehearsed by the actors. That was a sign of lazy writing. And nothing felt better than to make a room full of writers laugh at your joke. Well, except maybe when one of the four ladies at the table read laughed at something you wrote.

Another question I often get asked is, "Did you ever meet the actors?" No, Rose, we delivered the scripts in the dark of night, like "The Shoemaker and the Elves." Of course, we met them! We didn't spend a lot of time hanging out, but we saw them every day at rehearsals during tape weeks.

The other big question is, "Is it true that the ladies didn't get along?" Do you always get along with your coworkers? Or family, for that matter? And since they spent so much time together, they did become like family. So, of course they had their disagreements. But I think the first season, everyone was on their best behavior. And grateful to be on a giant hit.

I always say that of the four, Rue McClanahan was the most dedicated to the craft of acting. She took the character of "Blanche" very seriously. You absolutely knew she worked on Blanche's backstory. I remember when she approached a small group of us on set before they started a run-through.

Rue: "I wanna delve into what makes Blanche tick, so challenge me with strong stories."

Jim and I went back to our office and started thinking about what situations we could put Blanche in where she WOULDN'T want to have sex since that was her defining characteristic. That's how we came up with the plot of sexual harassment for "Adult Education," the second episode we wrote for the show. Unfortunately, we're still dealing with that kind of behavior from men in society.

January 20, 1986: *Work is going well. We can't believe how much of our material has stayed in so far on "Adult Education."*

I also couldn't believe that the network censors kept some of our racier lines, such as when Blanche tells off her teacher, Professor Cooper (see—an "er" at the end).

Blanche: "You sir, can kiss my *A*!"

But the most talked about line is in the scene where Blanche goes to Dean Tucker (another "er") to tell him about being sexually harassed.

Blanche: "Dean Tucker, what happened to me was really quite simple. I'm not doing very well in Professor Cooper's class, so he offered to give me an A, i-if I would . . ."

Dean Tucker hands Blanche a form. She looks it over.

Dean Tucker: "Do number five?"

Blanche: "Actually, number five, six, and seven-B."

Dean Tucker: "Why, that's terrible! Were there any witnesses?"

Blanche: "No."

Dean Tucker: "Oh. Oh. Well, that complicates things."

Blanche: "Why? Don't you believe me?"

Dean Tucker: "It's not a question of whether or not I believe you. It's just without substantial evidence, it's just your word against his, and a man's career is at stake!"

Blanche: "Well, so is mine, not to mention my dignity."

Dean Tucker: "I'm sorry. Look, I really am. I'd like to help you. But unfortunately, there's nothing I can do."

Blanche: "But that's not fair!"

Dean Tucker: "Miss Deveraux, life is not fair. I should know. I'm 43 years old, and until today, I never even heard of seven-B."

Blanche: "Well, I've known about it for some time, and as far as I'm concerned, you can go do it to yourself."

I've seen many exchanges in *Golden Girl* Facebook fan groups about what "seven-B" means. Since children may be reading this book, I'll simply say that the last line should give it away. But like good art, maybe we should leave the interpretation up to the viewer.

Regardless, I'm indebted to Rue for life. To this day, when working on episode ideas for a series, Jim and I will challenge our character's main personality traits. We find this always leads to compelling storylines. I'd like to believe that Rue came to talk to the writers because of her extensive theater training.

Oddly, we had some of that training in common. I didn't learn this until recently, but we both spent time at Hampton Playhouse—many years apart, of course. She was a professional union actor there, while I was merely a junior apprentice. I would have loved to have talked to her about that on set. We could've shared experiences about how theater changed our lives.

Luckily for audiences, Rue never forgot her roots and returned to the stage often. In fact, the last time I saw her was in a 2002 all-star production of Claire Luce's *The Women* on Broadway, alongside Cynthia Nixon (*Sex & the City*), Jennifer Coolidge (*White Lotus*), Jennifer Tilly (*Bullets Over Broadway*), and Kristen Johnston (*Third Rock from the Sun*).

Kind of makes your head spin!

I desperately wanted to go backstage after the show but was afraid she wouldn't remember me. She was fantastic in the play, but I felt bad that the costume designer put her in a slip that was too short for her to sit down in without exposing herself to the front row. That was downright cruel, as Blanche might say.

Years later, I read online about a *Golden Girls*-themed coffee shop in Washington Heights called Rue la Rue Café. On my next trip to NYC, I tracked down the owner and learned it was Michael de la Rue, a close friend of Rue's. Rumor has it that Rue had it put in her contract that she'd get to keep all of Blanche's clothes. She then left most of them to Michael, and he was planning to display them at the café.

I dragged my friend, Michael Urie (*Ugly Betty*) to visit the café with me. The minute we walked in the door, on the big screen TVs where de la Rue was screening episodes from shows, what should suddenly begin to play? My episode, "Adult Education"! Urie and I looked at each other, feeling like this place must be haunted. There is no way they knew the exact time we were arriving.

We were given the grand tour. They had spent a lot of money on all new appliances and design details, showcasing tons of memorabilia. It was adorable, and lots of fans came by, including Lin-Manuel Miranda, creator of the Broadway hit, *Hamilton*. He happens to be a super *Golden Girls* fan. Who knew?

But suddenly and mysteriously, the place closed after being open less than a year. Then I was most fortunate to get to know Rue through her sister, Melinda, who was also a guest on the Golden Fans at Sea cruises in February/March of 2020.

Melinda told hysterical stories about Rue with her Southern accent and flirty manner. Everyone on the ship fell in love with Melinda. She brought the brilliance of Rue back to life right before our eyes, even if for a brief moment in time.

What can I say about Bea Arthur? Intimidating? Hell, yeah. I was a big *Maude* fan and had great admiration for her. Of course, I also saw her in the filmed version of *Mame* with Lucille Ball. But we can forgive her for that. Any time in her presence would be an honor.

Except being in an elevator with her after a table read. I'm sure I was sweating buckets. It was the three of us: me, Jim, and a living legend. What does one do? I looked down at the floor. Big mistake. All I could see were her big feet in some kind of open-toed sandals. Supposedly, Bea hated wearing shoes, especially heels. In my mind, all I saw was two hairy feet with long nails, kind of like something from *Lord of the Rings*.

I'm sure they were lovely feet, but that's not what I saw at that moment of terror. I looked up and politely smiled, while silently praying that the elevator would move faster. No words were spoken. I don't think I could have formed any. Remember, we were young and green. I would later find out that Bea is very shy. She was probably feeling weird too—although *my* toes were completely covered.

I didn't think I could gain more respect for Bea Arthur, but I did during the week of the taping of the first episode we wrote, "Blanche and the Younger Man." A few days before we were to shoot in front of the live studio audience, Bea's mother died unexpectedly. The producers offered to postpone the taping. But much like Rue, Bea came from a theater background and said, "The show must go on!" She knew many jobs were at stake, and she would soldier on.

Everyone was so impressed. Especially during that kitchen scene, where Sophia thanks Dorothy for not treating her like a little girl but a person. If you look closely, you can see Bea start to tear up and have to look away from Estelle. You just know she's thinking about her mother. Even today, I get goosebumps when I watch that episode.

As much as I would have loved to have gotten to know Bea, we kept our distance. I often wondered if Estelle ever talked to her about us. I think Bea would've loved us. Especially since she was such a big supporter of gay rights. But that part of our lives was still never discussed at Sunset/Gower Studios.

At the wrap party, held at a mansion in Hancock Park, our production assistant and friend, Jeff Goodman, drove Bea home since she had been drinking. In the writers' room, we heard stories about how Bea would booze it up after work or at parties. But never on set. They said she was still hurting from a bitter divorce from her husband, Broadway director Gene Saks.

After we left the show, we didn't see Bea again until one weekday afternoon, years later. Jim and I were in Santa Monica at a matinee of Don Roos's cool indie film, *The Opposite of Sex*. We walked up to the box office to buy our tickets, and there were two older women in front of us. One of the voices sounded very low and familiar.

I looked down.

Open-toed sandals.

Holy crap! It was Bea Arthur. I nodded to Jim and mouthed her name and urged him to say something. I'm a good instigator. I almost had him saying something, then we saw who she was with—friggin' Angela Lansbury! Two "bosom buddies" out for a fun afternoon movie. They seemed a bit tipsy. In my mind, they met for lunch at the beach, had a few glasses of Chardonnay, then decided to catch a film. We purposely sat a couple rows behind them. The two cackled loudly at all the raunchy jokes. I'm not sure I saw much of the movie. I was too busy watching two old friends from their Broadway *Mame* days still enjoying each other's company.

I had one burning question: "Did these ladies drive themselves to the theatre?" I wouldn't have wanted to be behind them on the way home.

I wish I had gone to one of Bea's acclaimed solo shows. That's why we must grab those opportunities when they present themselves. The world brings them to your doorstep for a reason.

Now, onto Betty White. Growing up, I LOVED *The Mary Tyler Moore Show*, my favorite show on Saturday night. And I also loved the game show, *Password*, hosted by Betty's husband, Allen Ludden. "And the Password is . . ." (said in a stage whisper), still gets me to this day. Betty was always witty, a bit flirty, and great with a sharp comeback.

The moment I'm proudest of with Betty is in our "Blanche and the Younger Man" script. We saw a piece about her in the *New York Times* as we were writing our first draft. In the article, Betty talked about her deep love for her late husband. We put a quote of hers, word-for-word, in the script, changing Allen to Charlie (Rose's deceased husband).

Rose: "You know . . . after Daddy died, I just thought I'd never get over it. And Charlie . . . well, there's not a day goes by that I don't think about him."

The scene was so poignant, but knowing she was speaking her own words made it all the more so. We never told her or anybody on staff what we had done. Only Jim and I knew. And now you.

So, I'm sure everyone wants to know if the rumors were true. Did Bea and Betty hate each other? During our time on set, I never felt tension between the two. I only heard stories and recently learned, from producer Marsha Posner Williams on a podcast, that Bea thought Betty was two-faced. Bea liked real people. I had the sense that Betty was more like Sue Ann Nivens, the character she played on *The Mary Tyler Moore Show*, than she was like Rose. More conniving than the innocent airhead from St. Olaf.

Quick sidenote: St. Olaf was named during one of our episodes. I remember us all sitting around the room, going through the phone book (google that one too) and pitching names of different cities. We needed one that was funny but didn't sound too silly. St. Olaf is actually a real township located in Otter Tail County, Minnesota. It has a population of 430. Betty said in interviews that she was nervous the townspeople would think we were making fun of them. But supposedly they loved it and would send her gifts commemorating their village that was now known worldwide!

My view of Betty was colored by the way I saw her treat Estelle on set during tape nights. I really didn't like how when Estelle forgot a line, Betty would walk over to the studio audience and crack jokes at Estelle's expense, which seemed needlessly cruel. I wondered why she wasn't more sensitive to Estelle's feelings. Did Betty only care about animals and not people? Was a laugh that important?

Whatever the reason, I was protective of my friend Estelle. As she had been of me and Jim. Estelle had confided in me about her overwhelming anxiety during tape nights. It got so bad she had to go to therapy multiple times a week. In the writers' room, everyone thought she didn't know her lines because she was off at some Hollywood event all night long, enjoying her newfound celebrity, instead of being home learning her lines. What we didn't know was that she was starting to experience dementia. If you notice in certain scenes, Sophia will be eating raisins. That's because she's reading the lines that they wrote the lines on her hand.

For years I harbored resentment toward Betty about those tape nights. Especially when friends (or fans) would say how sweet she seemed. I'd plant a smile on my face, but I'm sure people saw through that. It's a funny thing; as you mature, you discover that everything isn't black and white. Now that I've learned more about who Betty was during her long career, that she didn't have a mean bone in her body, I think maybe she was trying to defuse the situation with humor so Estelle wouldn't feel bad about constantly flubbing up. Or maybe she was trying to keep the audience engaged and pumped up since tape nights can tend to drag on and on. Either way, this has taught me a lot about the first impressions we make on others. And how those impressions can evolve over time.

As with the other women, I had a full-circle moment with Betty. You get those the longer you live and the longer you last in the business. It occurred with Betty when I was shadowing director Andy Cadiff on the set for her TV Land show, *Hot in Cleveland*. I went to her dressing room to get my picture with her and remind her that I wrote on Season 1 of *The Golden Girls*. She smiled big, hugged me, and acted like she remembered. She was getting up in years at that time, but was still so funny and sharp with the ad-libs between takes. I'm glad I got up the nerve to ask her for that picture, which I will always cherish.

Later that day, producer Todd Milliner told me he was planning a big benefit for The Celebration Theatre, a local LGBTQ theater company he was on the board of. The Celebration also gave me my first theater directing gig. Todd wanted the cast of *Hot in Cleveland* to do a live reading of a *Golden Girls* script on the sound stage where *HIC* was filmed.

I immediately shot back, "Uh, duh. Why not use one of mine?! Like 'Blanche and the Younger Man.'"

He asked, "Can you email me a copy ASAP?"

I reminded him, "Todd, we wrote those scripts on typewriters. There were no such things as a PDF."

The next day I brought in my only copy. I carried it like a rare painting and gently handed it over to a PA to carefully make a copy.

On April 26, 2014, Stage 19 at CBS Radford Studio, we raised over $40k on a night I will never forget. And one that I didn't want to end. First, you should know that Betty refused to play "Rose." She insisted on reading the part of "Dorothy." I think she wanted to have fun and not recreate what she had already done. The cast included the always exceptional Wendie Malick as "Blanche," Valerie Bertinelli as "Rose," and a slightly miscast Jane Leeves as "Sophia." Others in the company were Max Greenfield as "Dirk" and Millicent Martin as Rose's mother, "Alma."

I was invited to watch a quick rehearsal/reading. As I listened, my heart was full. Even I questioned how such a complex script about women's issues came from the minds of such young writers. What were we thinking? It was so sensitive and specific. I was moved. As was the audience, especially during my pre-show speech. I told them the story about filming that episode during the week Bea's mother died.

On New Year's Eve, December 31, 2021, I was sitting in my living room, writing my "Year in Review" in my journal. My phone started buzzing with texts. I couldn't *not* look. I saw TMZ was reporting Betty had died. Was this for real? I checked online. It was. My social media was suddenly flooded with people shocked and speechless by the news. How could this happen? And mere weeks before her 100th birthday. You could feel a collective cry in the world.

Then my phone started ringing with requests from various news outlets. They wanted to know if I could go on live TV and talk about her. I wasn't sure I could. What would I say? Then it hit me. Betty wouldn't want people to be sad. She always had a smile on her face and a positive attitude. Maybe that's why she chose New Year's Eve to pass. This way, everyone would be together and they could toast her.

That night, I poured some vodka—Betty's favorite—and toasted her. Even at 99, we still wanted more from her. And somehow, she made us believe she would live forever. That day I saw she also had the capacity to bring people together, which she did for eight decades on TV, film, and stage. To make us all laugh. And when we did, we weren't red states or blue states. We were just Betty White states.

Now we come to my favorite *Golden Girl*—Estelle Getty. We were beyond thrilled when we knew we'd be getting to write for this gifted actress on a weekly basis. But the way she looked out for us from our first day on the set, I knew she was a special lady. I feel so fortunate to call her a friend. In fact, I think of her multiple times a week when I pass by her old apartment at 7560 Hollywood Boulevard, Apt. #406.

I especially remember the time she invited me over for one of her birthday parties. I was casually sitting on her couch, and in walk Betty White and Rue McClanahan. Together! For some reason, that accentuated how crazy my life had become. In the beginning, when Estelle would ask me to dinner, I'd get really excited, thinking I'd be having a private evening with this woman who was blowing up all over town. Then I'd get to the restaurant, and there'd be a table of twenty gay guys. Guys from all her companies of *Torch Song*. I was still thrilled to be included in her "family."

We did have one evening, just me and Estelle. She asked me to escort her to an AIDS fundraiser, which was a parody of *Fiddler on the Roof*, at a small theater in Hollywood. I jumped at the chance. I prized any moment we spent together or our talks on the phone. And felt honored that she confided in me about her stage fright every Friday tape night and having to go to therapy multiple times a week.

And then, at my big thirtieth birthday party, I looked over and thought I saw a small child. Upon closer inspection, I realized it was Estelle. I was so touched that she came to that event. I wish we could magically pick up where we left off, and I could hear her take on the world today. She was very wise and very opinionated. Much like the three women I grew up with. No wonder I felt so close to her.

My full-circle moment with Estelle came when I got the chance to speak to four people close to her. In the spring of 2020, I had this idea to write a one-woman play about Estelle Getty. I started by contacting two of her old managers, Juliet Green and Alan Siegel, who, at the time of *The Golden Girls*, owned a company called Green/Siegel. Estelle had been eager for Jim and me to meet them during Season One. "Trust me, you'll love them, and they'll love you."

She was right. They were around the set a lot since Estelle was basically alone in LA. Her husband was mysteriously living in Florida. (I never did meet him.)

By now, Alan and Juliet had ended their partnership, but both were happy to speak about Estelle. It brought me to tears when Juliet said how much Estelle adored me and Jim and always spoke fondly of us. I'd never heard that before.

I also didn't know about the complicated relationship Estelle had with her husband and children. Estelle's two sons are estranged, but I've gotten the chance to have long conversations with each of them separately. I learned about the dark sides of their family. To Estelle's credit, she never complained about her husband to me. She spoke about him kindly and simply said, "Arthur doesn't like all the 'glitz and glamour' of Hollywood. That's why he stays in Florida."

In reality, their relationship was pretty much over, and coming to LA for *The Golden Girls* gave Estelle an excuse to be on her own and pursue her dreams. She'd dreamed of acting for years, but the responsibilities of raising a family and taking care of a husband had made the pursuit difficult.

This created resentment on all sides. Especially with how to care for Estelle at the end of her life. Not to mention how hard it must've been for her sons to go out in public with everyone saying Estelle was like a grandmother to them when all they probably wanted was a "normal" mother at home. Not one who would make dinner, then disappear into Manhattan to do some crazy Off-Broadway show in a bra and slip.

One of those shows was *Torch Song Trilogy*. I heard stories about how Estelle saw her Broadway cast members getting sick with this new, mysterious illness. She'd bring home-cooked food, like chicken soup, to them in the hospital, not knowing how serious the disease was. She watched so many of her castmates fall prey to this horrible sickness. I think that's why it was so important for Estelle to go to any AIDS function she could and help raise as much money as possible. Strong women like her gave voice at a time when it was so desperately needed, and most actors (and politicians) were afraid to even say the disease's name out loud.

Writing for those four comedy titans at such an early age and such an early part of our careers will always be a highlight of my life. I was always conscious of being grateful for the experience *as* we were experiencing it. Not sure how I knew to hold those moments close to my heart, but I'm glad I did. Watching those women at work daily, you couldn't help but be inspired by their brilliance.

We tried to capture all of that in our third script, "The Flu." Although a fan favorite, especially during Covid, it was an extremely difficult episode to put together. We didn't have a normal A story and B story. This one had all four of them getting sick. And all four fighting. Rare for any series, but especially one in its first season. I think the producers knew it was going to be difficult, storytelling-wise, and I took it as a compliment that they trusted us with it. But then we handed in our first draft after doing exactly what they said to do.

FEBRUARY 5, 1986   JOURNAL ENTRY

Most of our script for "The Flu" is being scrapped. The staff and us will rewrite it in three days in the room. Sounds fun, huh? I thought we had done a good job. But some of the story line didn't work. The stuff they gave us! I still feel like a bit of a failure. I wish they would let us know if we will be back next season. This script is no indication.

Finally, we come to our last, but certainly not the least, *Golden Girl*. The exceedingly talented Susan Harris. As a student of TV, I looked up to her as a pioneer in the field of television writing and production, if only for creating *Soap*, a series way ahead of its time. For a young (closeted), gay man, I was thrilled and terrified when I watched the premier episode with my mom and the Epsteins during a trip to NYC. No one had ever seen a gay character like that on a network television show. I'd love to say I got to know Susan Harris well. But really, I only talked to her once (in person).

FEBRUARY 28, 1986   JOURNAL ENTRY

It's 1:46 a.m. I just returned from the wrap party for *Golden Girls*. Can you believe it's all over? Well, hopefully not all over. We've gotten such mixed messages. Terry, Kathy, Mort, Barry, and Wini Hervey seem to want us back. We introduced ourselves to Susan Harris, and twice she mentioned seeing us in two months. My fingers are crossed. We really need to have this happen. It seems to be a major stepping stone. After one more year, then anything is possible. This whole experience has been jam-packed with emotions. Each day changing. I know we've grown tremendously because of it. Thank you!!!!!!!!

We were exhausted but flying high. Somehow, we'd landed on the hottest TV show of the year. Of many years! We felt so lucky.

MARCH 13, 1986   JOURNAL ENTRY

After finishing Season 1, I went to see my mom in Santa Barbara, feeling good. We had gained a lot of confidence in ourselves. But on my return, I find out Paul and (especially) Tony do not want us back. They said they needed "more

heavyweights." Our contracts are not being renewed. Jim and I are beside ourselves. I think
they are making a big mistake. We brought a
lot to the show. Warmth, if nothing else. Paul
and Tony could not deal with us. They were
intimidated by us. It's getting boring—these
middle-aged men that are so insecure.

To quote Blanche Devereaux, "We were devastated, just devasted!"

It wasn't until a few years later that we learned from writers Mort Nathan and Barry Fanaro the real reason we weren't asked back for Season Two. At the beginning of the first season, Witt and Thomas had asked the staff to give their writer friend, Susan Beavers, a freelance episode while we were doing ours. Both scripts came in about the same time. For whatever reason, Susan's required major rewrites. Ours was more well received. It's no slight to Susan, who's a terrific writer. There are many reasons why certain scripts and writers work for certain shows.

I guess Paul's and Tony's egos were bruised, and they didn't like that "their person" wasn't the staff's choice to bring on for a full-time job. I sure hope it didn't have anything to do with us being gay.

My next encounter with Susan Harris occurred much more recently. On May 8, 2018, my home landline rang. Yes, I still have one since cell reception is not always great in the Hollywood Hills where I live. Caller ID said "UNLISTED." For some reason, I picked it up anyway.

I barely got out, "Hello," when this woman started screaming at me. I made out that it was Susan Harris. She was FURIOUS about *Silver Foxes*!

Let me explain what *Silver Foxes* is. The cable network, LOGO, called us in for a meeting and said they wanted to develop their first original sitcom. They spent months deciding who should write it and landed on us. I thought they were joking. But when I heard their show idea, a gay men's *Golden Girls*, it all made sense. We jumped at the chance and quickly closed a deal.

As we were polishing our first draft, I suggested we put together a reading in my living room to hear it out loud. We decided to go after our dream cast. Some actors we didn't know, like George Takei (*Star Trek*) and Leslie Jordan (*Will & Grace*), who instantly said *yes*. Without reading a script. The bar was set high, and every actor we contacted jumped in enthusiastically, including Bruce Vilanch, Todd Sherry, Melissa Peterman, Danielle Gaither, and Cheri Oteri.

I couldn't believe it. Neither could the network. They kept asking me, "How did you get all those great people in one room?"

I shrugged and said, "I just asked."

The reading went great. I even had our *Rita Rocks* producer, Franco Bario, attend so he could tell the network how they could inexpensively make a multi-cam show. In the end, it was still too costly for them. When we tried to get other networks to consider it, not one would even read it. A major streaming company said it didn't have "broad appeal." I read that as code for "It's too gay" and "Your characters are too old."

No matter how popular *Golden Girls* was (and still is) with ALL audiences, we couldn't find a buyer. Ageism and continued homophobia in Hollywood became a worldwide story. As did the picture of that star-studded reading.

Back to Susan Harris's angry phone call. It was hard to get a word in with her loud ranting, but I finally had to do something and blurted out, "Susan, please stop!"

She must've been shocked at my volume and took a breath.

I used that time to jump in: "In every interview I do, I always give you credit for creating such an amazing show, and I never say our show is a *Golden Girls* reboot. You of all people know how reporters use headlines as an easy way to attract readers to their articles."

She seemed to calm down, then softly said, "At least you had the courage to answer my phone call. Not like your coward of a writing partner."

I apologized for any misunderstanding and got off the phone as quickly as possible. I was shaking. I immediately called Jim. He wondered why his cell phone was ringing so much. He checked his voice mail and found a fifty-nine second message from a VERY irate Susan Harris. Here's the transcript. Never before revealed:

SUSAN HARRIS	PHONE MESSAGE

I assume this is James Berg. This is Susan Harris. In a number of publications, this has been written—"*Golden Girls* team to produce *Silver Foxes*. The team behind *Silver Foxes* was responsible for the cult classic, *Golden Girls*." You had NOTHING to do with *Golden Girls*. You wrote three episodes. The show was on seven years. Stop linking the two. I've got a lawyer on this. STOP IT! JUST STOP IT! Where are your morals to allow this to happen? I'M DISGUSTED! I'M OUTRAGED! You know that Paul died on Friday, and he would be as outraged as I was. JUST STOP IT!

I imagined her sitting in her huge mansion, all alone, grieving the recent death of Paul Witt, her husband/business partner. She goes to his funeral and has people coming up to her, congratulating her on her *Golden Girls* reboot.

I felt attacked, but I wasn't mad. More sorry for her, sensing the pain she was going through. And now without her husband.

Life after *The Golden Girls* wasn't terrible. Nobody seemed to ask why we weren't asked back. Everyone in the business knows politics sometimes plays a part in situations like that. Or maybe they knew Paul and Tony weren't easy to work with. Ultimately, it didn't matter. Being there for Season One changed everything for us. The show was a huge success. Loved by all ages. I can't think of another show like that.

Back in the day, they'd have *Golden Girls* viewing parties every

Saturday in West Hollywood bars. And yes, I would occasionally attend. Even at my grandmother's assisted living facility in suburban Detroit, I was a celebrity. She'd take me around to all the tables in the dining room, showing me off to her friends. And then the show got nominated for a bunch of Emmys. Not our "Rose's Mother" script. We lobbied to change the title from "Blanche and the Younger Man," thinking it sounded more award-worthy. But I was still happy for the show and proud to have been a part of it.

SEPTEMBER 21, 1986   JOURNAL ENTRY

Emmy Night! *Golden Girls* won Best Comedy. Mort Nathan & Barry Fanaro won for writing ("A Little Romance"). I have such mixed feelings. I wish I could let them go. I guess only time will heal them. Paul Witt mentioned all the directors, but not the writers. Also, Estelle lost. I was shocked. It would have been nice to be a part of the celebration. Maybe in years to come.

But then something completely unexpected happened when I was visiting New York.

FEBRUARY 28, 1987   JOURNAL ENTRY

At about 7:50 p.m. last night, Rande checked her machine for messages. We were waiting for Jim so we could all see *The Colored Museum* at the Public Theatre. She came back saying our agent called "urgent." I had no idea why. I ran to the pay phone. Jack Dytman's secretary wouldn't tell me anything.

She said, "This is the kind of thing your agent should tell you. But I promise it's good news."

Anyway, we were nominated for a WGA award for
Golden Girls ("Rose's Mother" episode). Can
you fucking believe it?! It was kind of hard
to enjoy the play after hearing that news. My
mind raced. We certainly got the last laugh.
Paul and Tony are going to be livid.

MARCH 13, 1987   JOURNAL ENTRY

I saw in Variety, that Paul, Tony, and
Touchstone took out two separate ads congratulating Terry Hughes on winning a DGA award
for *Golden Girls*. I want to win. And it will
be interesting to see if we get a similar ad.

We didn't.

MARCH 29, 1987   JOURNAL ENTRY

Went to the WGA Awards with Julie Silverman.
Jim took Fred and Ruth Horne. The dinner/cer-
emony was very long, but very exciting. The
best part was driving there. I felt great. I
looked great. I couldn't believe I was going
to an awards show in Hollywood . . . and I was
being honored. Quite thrilling! I was a bit
let down when they didn't call our name. But
also a bit relieved. I never saw us winning.
I couldn't help it, but that was what I saw.
Estelle was great to see, and she said she
stayed for our category. So sweet of her. The
other women left after presenting an award.

Besides having all these wonderful "Full-Circle Moments" with
each "Girl," I started to have them with the show in general. Whenever
I'd go to a gay bar over the years, I'd meet young guys who could recite

lines from our scripts. They would tell me how they'd watch the show with their grandmothers. At first that made me feel old, but lately I love hearing stories like that.

Of course, now they watched the reruns on Hallmark, TV Land, and Hulu, not the original airings. And then I started noticing waves, where the popularity of the show would suddenly get even bigger, if that's possible. I think I first noticed it when they started doing line-by-line productions of the actual episodes performed by guys in drag. Or original shows using the characters from the series. Even puppet versions.

I've gotten to be on many *Golden Girls* podcasts and panels, attend Golden-Con, the pop-up restaurant, sit on a rattan couch at D3 (the big Disney convention in Anaheim), and go on board The Golden Fans at Sea cruises. The fans are always so kind and often apologize for wanting to talk to me or ask questions. I tell them, unlike actors, writers rarely get to meet fans. It's so cool to hear stories of what the show meant to them.

One story really touched me. A young woman, who was going through a terrible time with cancer, had to have another operation. As she was being wheeled into the operating room, the nurse saw she was carrying an iPod with earbuds. She wanted to listen to Andrew Gold's memorable *Golden Girls* theme song to keep her company. The nurse felt bad. She couldn't allow the iPod in the operating room because it wasn't sterile. But inside the room, right before this woman was put under, she looked up and the entire staff of doctors and nurses started singing, "Thank you for being a friend."

I heard so many beautiful stories like that. How the show helps people get through tough times. When we were mere "children" writing on the show, we never thought about impacting people that way or the legacy it would have. But I sure am thinking about it now. Kind of hard not to with viewership at an all-time high and all of the crazy *Golden Girls* merchandise out there.

We were too busy wondering if we'd ever work again.

5

LIFE AFTER THE LADIES

N ot being asked back to *Golden Girls* was hard on the ego. But the upside was we were now considered "in-demand" writers. We had back-to-back staff jobs that finally enabled us to move up the ladder in job titles. For many television seasons, we'd have offers on multiple series.

We didn't always choose wisely.

There's nothing better than when your agent calls saying someone read your scripts and wants to meet you. One such call came regarding a new ABC sitcom adaptation of Ron Howard's comedy, *Gung Ho*. Our mentor, Gary Keeper, had taught us it's always good to enlarge your network of fans, so off we went for an interview with John Rappaport (*MASH*), the executive producer/showrunner.

I remember sitting on the couch across from him in his office at Paramount. The interview was going great; then he says, "So, you guys are Violets?"

Jim and I froze. Beads of sweat started to form around my hairline. I thought he was asking us if we were gay. But why would he use that word? And how could he tell?

I think he saw the panic on our faces and quickly clarified that the "Violets" is the name for the sports teams at NYU.

First off, NYU had sports teams?! News to us.

Times were starting to change, and gays and lesbians were finally starting to flex their political muscles. So, when we got the gig, we decided to come out to the staff. We felt safe to finally acknowledge who we really were. It was VERY liberating.

But sadly, the staff consisted of ALL white, straight, male writers. Except for us. And of course, we gravitated toward the female writers' assistants, especially Ruth Horne. She told us that one day when Jim and I were in our office working on a script, the rest of the male staff came up with a hypothetical: If they were stranded on a desert island (why is it always a desert island?) and they had to have sex with me or Jim, which would they pick?

I got the exec producer, so I feel like I won.

I was still awfully young on that show, and sometimes I'd blurt out things that today, I may let stay in my head. Like, I kept asking, "Why are the two lead characters friends?"

A honest and, I think, intelligent question. But the more seasoned writers didn't take it that way. They thought, *Who is this punk kid questioning our writing?! Just put in some jokes and move on.* I wanted to make the show deeper and better. Some of them only wanted the scripts to be finished.

We had little interaction with Ron Howard. Or the movie writers, Lowell Ganz and Babaloo Mandel. When they did come in, they'd fight with John. The scripts went through extensive rewrites. Oftentimes we'd have to work seven days a week. Weekends we'd be stuck at John's house way out in the Valley.

But we got to do some cool things on the show. Like, I was the one who suggested then-newcomer Scott Bakula to replace the lead actor from the pilot. Scott was a super-talented guy, and I'm so happy he's had such a long career on multiple hit series.

There was another part of my job I'm proud of, even though I'm sure I was considered annoying again. I found it offensive that the female characters' physical attributes were usually the only characteristics they were given. I'd say, "Can't we describe her more than simply saying she's pretty?"

AUGUST 21, 1986   JOURNAL ENTRY

Work on *Gung Ho* has been exhausting. But the
nice thing is we are really appreciated and
recognized for our talent. The complete opposite of our experience on *Golden Girls*.

JANUARY 23, 1987   JOURNAL ENTRY

Good news—*Gung Ho* was canceled. I was so mis-
erable at work. I'd leave my house determined
to go the office with a positive attitude,
but the minute I drove through the gates at
Paramount, I felt a dark cloud come over me.
Two weeks ago, Jim and I had an intense talk
in his backyard. He told me that we have to be
at work, we have a contract, so I need to make
the best of it. Find the joy. Whatever that
took. Those words really clicked for me. Since
then, things have been easier. Thank you, Jim,
for that life lesson!

After *Gung Ho* ended, our agent said my comments in the room
made me seem like I had "an attitude." Uh, yeah! An attitude against
sexist writing. I was told that "attitude" cost us a job on Jeff Franklin's
new show, *Full House*. We lost a big gig. I felt bad and apologized to
Jim. But now I wear that as a badge of honor. And Mary Kate and
Ashley Olsen did fine without us.

Even though we were not having the best experiences on show
staffs, we *were* having the time of our lives in Los Angeles. In the 80s,
the city was a wild world to behold. I had a few bucks saved up from
all those TV gigs and could now afford to go to some of the hippest
restaurants of the moment—Linda's, I Love Juicy, Kate Mantalini's,
City Thai, and my favorite, Muse. That was "the" place to be seen and
hobnob from table to table with all the young, fabulous, up-and-coming

gays and lesbians. And after dinner, we'd all go to exclusive clubs like Flaming Colossus, Boys & Girls, and The Pink.

My friend, Jim Budman, co-owned The Pink in Santa Monica. I met Sandra Bernhard there. Actually, in their parking lot. We instantly hit it off. I knew of her from her dynamic film debut in Martin Scorsese's *King of Comedy*. I found her to be brilliant, insightful, and so smart. And of course, hysterical. Others were scared of her. To me, she seemed like a nice Jewish girl I would've been friends with at temple or in high school. And we were both from Michigan.

Jim and I sold a pilot idea for a limited series to Showtime called *Sandra Bernhard: Trapped in a Movie of the Week!* Back then, TV movies were all the rage, and we thought it would be funny to see Sandra play a neurotic young woman who each week falls into a different genre of TV movies. In the pilot, her character was such a hypochondriac, she came down with every illness from all those overly dramatic disease-of-the-week films.

Right before Sandra went to NYC for her first big Off-Broadway show, *Without You I'm Nothing*, she asked me to a goodbye dinner at a Chinese restaurant on Pico Boulevard. I was surprised by the invite. We were at the very beginning of our friendship. I was nervous because I didn't know any of her friends. I went anyway. She sat me next to her writer friend from Toronto, Elaine Pope (*Seinfeld*).

I barely got my coat off, and Elaine suddenly blurted out to me, "So, how much money do you make?" We've been really good friends ever since.

I went to NYC multiple times while Sandra was performing at the Orpheum Theatre on Second Avenue in the East Village. She had me pick her up at the theater after the show. I would purposely arrive a little early so I could hear her belt out the closing song, which became her anthem—a rocking cover of Prince's "Little Red Corvette." I still think of her whenever I hear the first few bars of that song.

After the show, we'd walk through the Village and talk, sometimes grab a late-night snack. I'd have a drink; she'd have tea. I don't think I ever saw her drink liquor. Then I'd walk her to her West Village sublet. She was renting model Tatiana's place at No. 1 Christopher Street.

One night when we got to the lobby of the apartment, she said, "You have to come upstairs and hear the message I got on my answering machine today."

For you kids, an answering machine was a device that would take phone messages if someone called and no one was home. This was before you could call in and hear those messages. You had to wait until you got home to see who called. All very suspenseful.

That night, I could tell Sandra was excited to share who called her. We sat on her bed and she pressed "play." It was a message from Madonna, who'd tracked down Sandra's number and wanted to hang out with her. Sandra asked me what she should do.

Without hesitation, I said, "I'm leaving. Call her back and go hang out with her!"

She did. They did. And suddenly they were besties and making appearances everywhere together. Even on *Late Night with David Letterman*, which fueled rumors of a possible romantic relationship. There wasn't one. But I think they both liked messing with the public and didn't go out of their way to deny it.

NOVEMBER 20, 1988   JOURNAL ENTRY

I went to the opening of *Hurlyburly* starring Sean Penn on Wednesday with Budman at the Westwood Playhouse. I hung out with Sandra at the after-party. She introduced me to Madonna. Sandra asked me to drive her home and as we left, we were chased to my car by paparazzi. It was really strange. But I must admit, I kind of enjoyed it. I wonder if I'll ever be that famous.

Years later, I had another encounter with Madonna. It was at this tiny dive bar on Pico Boulevard called Club Louis, run by actor/director Steve Antin (*Burlesque*). I was dancing the night away with Sandra and our group of power gays. Suddenly there was a hush in the place.

"Madonna's here!"

"Madonna and Warren Beatty."

Warren, Madonna's boyfriend at the time, sat patiently in the corner, letting Ms. Ciccone "get into the groove" on the dance floor with all of us.

Somehow, I found myself in the women's bathroom, just me, Sandra, and Madonna. I sat on the sink counter; don't ask me why. Not very hygienic. In a lame attempt to get on Madonna's good side, I joined her in making fun of Sandra, as only good gal pals do. And we all bonded. Or at least we did in my mind. A once gawky kid, now living life to his fullest in Los Angeles.

While Sandra was spending more and more time in New York, Elaine Pope and I were fast becoming close friends. In fact, closer than me and Sandra. I have been most fortunate to be Elaine's "Plus One" at many fabulous parties over the years, like Carrie Fisher's (*Star Wars*) and Penny Marshall's (*Laverne & Shirley*) infamous, celebrity-packed parties. Carrie and Penny took turns hosting their yearly, high-profile gatherings. Elaine had been partnered with Carrie when they both had development deals at Universal.

The first of these parties took place at Carrie's sprawling home in Beverly Hills. It had rolling gardens and an old-school Hollywood vibe. Which made sense since Bette Davis used to live there. Every time I turned around at the bar or in line at the buffet, I saw a famous movie star. The type that would be in a Hollywood Wax Museum.

At Penny's house in the Hollywood Hills, not far from my house, I got to see Penny's glass-encased collection of signed baseballs and basketballs. She was an avid sports fan and collector. Elaine had a good plan: grab some of the delicious gourmet food and park ourselves on a couch directly opposite the front door. There we'd have a front row seat to a parade of stars, like Tom Hanks, Meg Ryan, Jim Carrey, Renée

Zellweger, Barry Diller, David Geffen, Naomi Campbell, Sally Field, George Lucas, Francis Ford Coppola, John Travolta, Mike Meyers, Nicole Kidman, Cindy Williams, Steve Martin, and of course, Garry Marshall. Real A-listers.

And then the brightest star entered: Debbie Reynolds (*Singin' in the Rain*—one of my all-time favorites). The minute she burst through the door, you could tell why she was so successful in Hollywood for so many decades. She made a beeline for us since Elaine had written *These Old Broads*, a hysterical TV movie starring Debbie, Elizabeth Taylor, and Joan Collins. When Debbie learned I was a writer, she quickly started digging in her purse and proceeded to hand me a book of matches with her name embossed on it. Anyone could give out business cards. Not Debbie Reynolds.

If that wasn't memorable enough, Elaine took me to one of the best parties I've ever attended in Hollywood—the 2004 Vanity Fair Post-Oscar party. Elaine was invited since she had cast Graydon Carter, the publisher of Vanity Fair, in her feature film remake of *Alfie*.

Smart woman.

Once the ceremony was over on TV, she had me meet her a few blocks from Morton's Restaurant in West Hollywood, where the annual party took place. I hopped into her car, and then she drove a few blocks west, where security was on high alert. The valet took her car, and we headed in. It was crazy to have watched the show not twenty minutes prior, then suddenly be standing face-to-face with all these celebs in the exact designer outfits I'd seen them in at home, when I was in sweats.

Everyone was super nice and treated us like old friends. It felt as if there was a secret understanding. If you were powerful enough to snag an elusive invite to the most famous soirée of the year, you must be somebody worth talking to.

The first person we met while waiting at the bar for a drink was Faye Dunaway (*Network*). She was sweet as could be. Nothing like all of the horror stories everyone's heard. It's no wonder since we revealed that we were both comedy writers. Faye was desperate to show her funny side and wanted us to write her something. We played along, knowing this was a once in a lifetime opportunity to be standing shoulder to shoulder with a true Hollywood diva.

Eventually, we politely excused ourselves, saying that Elaine had to look for Jude Law and Sienna Miller, the stars of her film (and then a couple). While on the hunt for the gorgeous Brit couple, we passed everyone, including Oscar winners Charlize Theron and Sean Penn. I even forced myself to chat with Lindsay Lohan.

The most exciting person to see at any party is Oprah Winfrey. She radiates. I even ran into my neighbor (at the time) and actor/friend, Christine Taylor, "Marcia" from *The Brady Bunch Movies*. She was excited to see me. And have someone to talk to. We were laughing and having a grand old time, and then her husband, Ben Stiller, came running over, acting all jealous. Like I was trying to put the moves on his lady. He seemed to chill out when he found out who I was. I most certainly was not hitting on his wife. But I would do anything to work with her again.

Having lived in LA for so many years, I've had the privilege of going to many wonderful events. An extremely memorable one comes to mind. My friend Peter brought me to one hosted by the then-couple Catherine Keener (*The 40-Year-Old Virgin*) and Dermot Mulroney (*My Best Friend's Wedding*). It was a small, intimate gathering. Ellen DeGeneres was there, but my eyes were fixated on Brad Pitt, accompanied by his girlfriend at the time, a pre-Goop Gwyneth Paltrow. I didn't shower for a week after Brad hugged me goodbye.

I got to go to a few Clive Davis parties at the famous Beverly Hills Hotel. He'd rent the same bungalow every time he'd come to Los Angeles. Jim Budman is close friends with Clive and snagged me an invitation. I found him fascinating and such a generous, sweet man. I was also fascinated with his story of being a self-made businessman with an uncanny ear and eye for budding music legends.

My best experience with Clive was when I arrived at the suite, and he grabbed me by my hand and whisked me to a private room. He was very excited about a music video he'd recently shot for his new recording artist, Whitney Houston. The song was "I Want to Dance with Somebody." He wanted me to watch it and then hear MY opinion. No pressure there. I watched it. Naturally, I LOVED her voice, look, and obvious star quality. She absolutely had "it."

I did have one note. I was hesitant about bringing it up, but he encouraged me to say whatever I thought.

Me: "I think it's missing a story being told." It was the writer in me talking. Or the vodka. "Maybe you could try bookending it." I had to explain that term.

Me: "It's something you add at the beginning and end of a piece to give it some context. Make it more story-driven, so you feel for the main character."

He nodded, taking that in, then we rejoined the party.

Well, wouldn't you know when the video finally came out, it was "bookended." Nobody ever said anything. But deep down, I will always know that I'm responsible for Whitney's huge career. Kidding. (Well, maybe just a little.)

The biggest, most life-changing party that Budman got me invited to was one of Allee Willis's famous parties at her home, which was once the MGM party house. I didn't know who she was, but once he started listing her song credits, like Earth, Wind & Fire's "September" and "Boogie Wonderland," I was more than a little intrigued.

How can I explain my long and wonderful relationship with Allee? It might be best if we start at the end. Of her life. With the eulogy speech I was asked to give at her memorial service. Here's an excerpt of what I said in front of Allee's celebrity friends. With much difficulty, on December 26, 2019, at Mount Sinai Memorial Park:

IN A GALAXY FAR, FAR AWAY, the early 80s, my friend Jim Budman, said I had to meet him at this big party in the

Valley. But first I had to get "approved" by the hostess—that would be Allee. I had two things going for me. One, I was from Detroit, just like her. And second, I was a writer on this new, little TV show called The Golden Girls. I was in!

I put on a cute, polyblend outfit and headed over the hills to Otsego Street in the distant land known as Valley Village. I didn't realize that would be the first of a gazillion drives to the famous pink house.

Allee and I hit it off instantly. I made her laugh. That deep, hearty laugh of hers that could fill a room. My life was complete. At the end of the night, I was thrilled when she asked for my phone number.

Months later, I was sitting at my house on a Saturday afternoon, and the phone rang. It was Allee. I was surprised to hear from her since we hadn't spoken since that party. She was calling from a Vegas hospital. She had driven her van to Linda and Larry Hart's house for a big weekend event and had gotten food poisoning. She asked if I was free to come get her and drive her back home.

I don't know what came over me, but the first words out of my mouth were, "I'll be on the next plane out." Suddenly I'm at Burbank Airport heading to Sin City! When I got to the hospital, (it was actually in a temporary trailer in back), they were undoing Allee's IV, and she was ready to be released.

The next day I drove Allee home, through the desert, in her huge van. We laughed our asses off, with her stretched out in the back. I told her I had never been to Vegas before. Of course, she was horrified and immediately promised to take me back, her treat, on an extraordinary, super-duper tour of Las Vegas—The Allee Willis Way!

Over the decades of our fun-filled friendship, I'd often joke with her, "So, uh, when am I finally gonna get that trip?"

To be honest, I cared more about spending time with her than seeing Vegas. Being in her company was always a treat.

If there's any takeaway from the sadness of the past few days, it's that it's reminded me, in very stark terms, to not wait. If there's something you want to do, do it! Something you want to say, say it! Can be as simple as texting (or God forbid, calling them). Not for any special reason, just to say, "I'm thinking of you. Have a great day!"

Or maybe it's to make a commitment, to ourselves and to Allee, to finally take that extraordinary, super-duper tour of Las Vegas before it's too late.

It was so hard trying to get through that without collapsing into a puddle of tears. What really helped was looking out into the chapel full of Allee's friends and coworkers and seeing the beautiful face of Cinderella looking up at me with tears in her eyes. Okay, not literally Cinderella. It was Lesley Ann Warren (1965 TV production of *Cinderella*). Pretty much the same thing.

So many people came up to me after and thanked me for that beautiful tribute to Allee. They said I really captured the essence of her. I'm glad her girlfriend, Prudence Fenton (*Liquid Television*), forced me to do it after I begged her to pick one of Allee's friends who were more used to the spotlight. Prudence said Allee would've wanted me. So, somehow, I found the strength (and the words) to express my deep feelings for such a special person in my life.

What more can I say about Allee? Her fashion sense, her art, the 50s furniture and mid-century design of her house. I had never seen anything like it. Or like her. She had long hair on one side of her head and it was cropped short on the other. She had a tough, intimidating exterior. But oddly enough, I wasn't intimidated. Quite the opposite.

Allee and I became close friends after that trip to Vegas to collect her. She loved that I "got her." She said most people didn't. She introduced me to the world of thrift shopping beyond clothes. Home decorations and knickknacks.

Once, by chance, we ended up in Detroit at the same time. It was an opportunity to tour the city I had grown up in, but through her eyes. We even drove to her childhood house. Much to my surprise, she got nervous like a little girl and didn't want to knock on her old front door. That was so unlike her. She always seemed fearless to me. I wasn't having it. I told her we'd come all this way; we're not leaving until she did. I knew this was emotional for Allee, so I let her have her space and waited patiently in the car.

She went up on the porch and knocked. A man answered and let her in. She wasn't inside long, but when she came back out, she had a huge smile on her face. She said her bedroom was smaller than she remembered. The current owner was excited to meet her, so she promised him a longer visit the next time she was in town. I felt good for urging her to face her fears.

Over the years, Allee and I had so many wonderful experiences. She became family to me. So did Prudence when she came into Allee's life. At first, I didn't understand their relationship. How could you date someone and NOT want to live together? But I soon saw what finding your soulmate meant. And that every person can define it differently.

Allee made me expand my mind in so many ways. I think I had the same effect on her. She knew in me she had someone she could always count on, no matter what. And I knew she respected me and my talent. That's why when she got the opportunity to audition to write songs for a proposed Broadway musical of *The Color Purple*, I was one of the first calls she made. She hated Broadway and musicals and didn't really know the music of the time period the show took place in. I have such a vast music collection (LPS, CDs, and, yes, even cassette tapes), that I grabbed as much as I could carry and headed over to her house. She did her research and was working with two terrific songwriting partners, Brenda Russell ("Piano in the Dark") and Stephen Bray. I was friends with the show's producer, Scott Sanders, and happened to be visiting him at his summer home in Amagansett when he received their sample songs. He was bursting with excitement to play them for me. He was relieved that he liked them so much. They got the gig!

I've seen the show MANY times over the years. First, at Atlanta's Alliance Theatre for their initial tryout. Then in NYC for the big Broadway opening, December 1, 2005. Allee had her close friends meet her outside the theater where David Letterman filmed his late night talk show. Oprah was making a special appearance on his show, and he was going to walk her down the street (on camera) to the Broadway Theatre since she was one of the producers. It was a huge night for Allee, and I felt so proud to have a seat up close to witness it.

Later that year, when Allee went East for the Tony Awards, I suggested her friends all meet and watch the Tonys live at her house. Sometimes I have good ideas. We went nuts when LaChanze won! We were all so happy for our Allee.

Allee had an energy, a spirit, that I've never seen in any human being. It was always fun being around her. I loved having group experiences with her because she knew such interesting and accomplished people. But I especially loved our private moments. And I loved seeing her becoming more open and emotional during the last few years. She was really proud of me when she'd come to one of my plays and always bragged about me to her friends. Coming from her, that meant so much. And then she started saying "Love you" whenever I'd leave her house after an evening together. I'm not sure where that was coming from, but after hearing those words, I'd skip to my car and drive home with a huge smile on my face. And a warm feeling in my heart.

I thought I'd have many more years hearing that. But then, on December 24, 2019, I was at my friend Susannah Blinkoff's glamorous, new, modern house in Pasadena for a big Christmas Eve party. My phone buzzed with a call. I looked down. It was Paul Reubens, aka Pee-wee Herman. I'd met him through Allee, and we became good friends, even though he and Allee had a MAJOR falling out. I thought he was merely wishing me a Merry Christmas, so I didn't answer. Then he texted and said to call. I thought he was being silly. But something compelled me to call back. The partygoers had assembled in the living room around a piano where Susannah was starting to lead them in raucous singing of Christmas carols. I found a side office and ducked in there for some privacy.

Paul answered the phone. He didn't mince words. He blurted out, "Allee died."

I froze. I didn't understand.

He started to explain, "She wasn't feeling great during an after-dinner walk in her neighborhood with Prudence last night, so they went to the hospital. They did some tests but didn't find anything. She was literally putting on her shoes to leave the hospital, and her eyes went back in her head. And then her heart stopped."

So did my breathing. I was speechless. Too numb to cry. But I knew I had to get home. Immediately. I frantically searched for a way out through the back of the house. There wasn't any. My lone exit was through the living room, where everyone was cheerfully singing, to the front door.

Susannah, sitting at the piano, caught my eye. She mouthed, "Are you alright?"

I shook my head.

She came over to me, and I whispered, "Allee died. I have to get home."

Susannah is an exceptionally talented singer/songwriter, and I had taken her to see Allee's one-woman show a few years prior. She knew how much Allee meant to me. And the world. She hugged me and sent me on my way.

I'm not sure how I made it home, but I did. I still find it hard to look at pictures of Allee. I think I'm still in shock.

What has been somewhat cathartic, but also very emotional, is working on *Long Beach Blanket Bingo,* a new theater musical play I'm writing with Jim. Prudence was nice enough to give us access to Allee's vast catalog. Spending the summer of 2020 listening to recordings of all her demos and hearing her talk, it was as if she were alive again. It was wild, eavesdropping on her creative music sessions with such legends as Jimmy Cliff, James Brown, Maurice White, and others. But also, I had tinges of guilt, feeling maybe I shouldn't be doing this. Is it too personal, like reading her diary?

Then Allee's assistant said she wanted someone to go through all her old material and make new art. She actually verbalized that. And that's what I hope to do with this project. And to keep Allee's legacy alive.

One of Allee's good friends was Lily Tomlin. My love affair with Lily began as a kid in Detroit. The minute she appeared on the hit variety show, *Laugh-In*, I fell hard. *Laugh-In* was this crazy, funny, very topical, and wildly colorful show in the late 1960s-early 70s. Lily came on the show in Season Two and introduced the world to her brilliance through such vivid characters as the wise child, Edith Ann, and the persnickety phone operator, Ernestine.

I was instantly intrigued because she was also from Detroit. But she got out and went to Hollywood and was now starring on the biggest, most influential show of its time. And there was something about her. I couldn't put my finger on it, but I felt this intense bond with her. I even wrote her a fan letter and mailed it to her at NBC Studios in "Beautiful Downtown Burbank." I was over the moon when she sent me back a signed card with her photo on it. I still have it.

Then I read in the paper that she was going to be signing her first comedy album at Hudson's Department Store at Northland Mall, not far from our house. My mother knew there'd be no living with me if we didn't go. So, she took me, and we waited in line for Lily to sign my record. I still have that too.

One of the coolest things my mom ever did was take me and my sister to Cobo Hall in downtown Detroit to see Lily perform at a NOW meeting. Yes, NOW, as in the National Organization for Women. At that time, the Women's Movement was gaining steam but was still controversial in the Midwest. My mother told my father she was taking us to a Lily Tomlin concert. On the long walk in, I remember her holding my and my sister's hands and explaining that there would be mostly women there. And a lot of these women were probably lesbians. And how they were an important part of the burgeoning Women's Movement, although some women didn't think that was a good idea. A complex, yet honest, explanation.

Mom was very interested in politics and current events. In fact, we'd often have our little black-and-white kitchen TV on during dinner with the nightly network news playing. This would inevitably lead to smart, lively discussions on the hot news topic of the day. Even at an early age, I appreciated that she talked to us like people, not like little kids. And she nurtured whatever each of her kids had a passion for. Mine was anything Lily Tomlin.

So, there we were, probably the only two children in this vast indoor arena. And now it makes so much sense to me why I feel more comfortable around women, especially lesbians. I'm sure my father blamed my mother for the way I turned out. I thank her.

I'm also sure my mother got an earful after my father was humiliated at my performance in an elementary school talent show. Even though I got the biggest laughs and applause of anyone in the entire show. Okay, here's a confession I've NEVER admitted publicly. Not on any podcast or even to close friends. Except for Jim Berg.

I desperately wanted to be a part of our school's talent show; I think I was in fourth or fifth grade. I had the crazy idea that I would impersonate Lily's famous telephone operator character, Ernestine, in the show. Not a witch or warlock as I would do years later. But in full drag—wig, dress, makeup, everything. In front of the whole school. Students, parents, and families were invited. For a closeted boy in the Midwest back then, I must've been out of my mind. I truly don't know where I got the nerve. And although I loved the laughs I received, I must've felt shame because I've never talked about that in a public situation. Internalized homophobia is deep-seated and toxic. But for those few minutes on stage, when I was chortling and saying, "One ringy dingy," just like Lily's "Ernestine," I was in heaven.

Years later, I told Lily about imitating her in drag. Her response was, "Of course you did!"

As a kid who dreamed of having dinner with Lily Tomlin, I can now say I've broken bread with her numerous times.

The first feature film Jim and I decided to write after our initial burst of success in TV was a script called, *The Ruthie Ruddick Story*. We attended one of the first Gay and Lesbian Film Festivals in LA, where we saw this amazing documentary called *Before Stonewall*. In the movie, they spoke about how the Women's, Black, and Gay movements all collided in the summer of '69. After, in the theater lobby, Jim and I talked about how intriguing that was and thought it would be a great idea for a film. Now, if we could figure out a character who could intersect all those movements.

We started excitedly brainstorming, and by the time we got to our cars, we had come up with Ruthie Ruddick, a fictional suburban housewife who goes to Greenwich Village in the summer of 1969 to save her sister from becoming a hippie. In the process, she runs smack into those three movements and inadvertently starts a few trends along the way—like tie-dyeing, bra-burning, and the Stonewall riots. Mind you, this was BEFORE *Forrest Gump*.

We thought our agent wouldn't want us to waste time with writing such a gay-themed film. So, we didn't tell him and wrote it on the side. When we were done, we knew we had something special. And there was one person who had to play "Ruthie"—Lily Tomlin. We hoped Lily would relate to our movie's theme about acceptance of ALL people. But how would we get it to her? Just like Leonard Finger had taught me to figure out a way to get to a famous actor, I did.

I suggested to Jim, "What if we hire a messenger to deliver our script to her stage door? She's performing her one-woman show, *Appearing Nightly,* at the Doolittle Theatre now."

We wrote a doozy of a note and sent it off. We almost forgot about it until two weeks later when our agent called and asked, "Why is Lily Tomlin calling my office?"

Oops.

We had to confess what we had done. At that point, it didn't matter. Lily LOVED our script and wanted to meet us.

Back then, you sent a script out "wide," meaning to major producers with studio deals for "Weekend Read," desperately hoping for at least one or two potential buyers. By Monday morning, we had a bidding war from Hollywood production companies headed by Ron Howard, Eddie Murphy, John Davis, etc. We settled on John Davis, and he arranged a dinner for me and Jim to bond with Lily.

JULY 2, 1987   JOURNAL ENTRY

Just got back from dinner with Lily Tomlin at Columbia Bar & Grille. (John Davis and Darlene Chan, his development exec, came later.) I think the three of us really got along. Similar senses of humor. So rare. I'm sure she felt the same. Hopefully Monday we can start a bidding war between Universal, Lorimar, Warner, and UA. After, Jim and I called our loved ones and peed on the street in Hollywood.

That's right, we actually urinated behind the restaurant. That's because Jim and I made a pact. Neither of us were allowed to get up to use the bathroom during dinner and leave the other alone with Lily. We were that intimidated. I remember she used the word "epiphany." I had never heard that word and simply nodded and hoped all of my expensive NYU acting training would pay off. It must have because Lily attached herself to the project, and John sent out the script to all the major studios.

The script ended up at Universal with a huge price tag and really put us on the map as hot, new screenwriters. Having Lily involved helped enormously because she is so well-respected in town. Really, in any town. Although I got the sense that she didn't realize the power she had in Hollywood. Or know how to wield it. Perhaps it had something to do with the backlash she encountered after starring in and producing *Moment by Moment*, a romantic comedy film costarring John Travolta that her lover, Jane Wagner, directed.

Since we were getting notes from Lily on our script, we got to go on the set of *Big Business*, a terrific comedy she made with Bette Midler, and have our meetings there. That's when a real friendship started to develop. It was such a high to see her on Larry King's CNN show and mention our script as her next movie project. And the studio was loving our rewrites. Especially the speed at which we could hand in new drafts. I think it was our TV training. Then things got serious as the talk turned to who should direct. Actor Henry Winkler was getting great buzz after a movie he was directing with Billy Crystal, *Memories of Me,* was being successfully screened for people in the biz. So off we went to meet him.

JUNE 2, 1988   JOURNAL ENTRY

The meeting with Henry Winkler is over. Thank God! We hated the way he ridiculed our "bra burning" scene and how he wants us to "do our homework" about the 60s. Anyway, the studio likes him, and we want to see our movie get made—the bottom line is we will make it work. The experience is too valuable. Even though we get the sense that he feels we're too young to write about those turbulent times. We've got to prove him wrong.

We took Henry's comments as a challenge and set out to study the time period. In depth. We even arranged a session with 60s activist Tom Hayden. He was married to Jane Fonda at the time, so we got to go to their house in Santa Monica to interview him. It was so cool. In one room, we're peppering him with questions about protesting, and in the other, she's having a high-powered meeting with multi-Oscar musician John Williams. You know, just your average working married couple.

In typical Hollywood fashion, our script now sits on a shelf somewhere with too much money against it to ever get made. I still hold out hope that some big female star will read it and demand to play "Ruthie Ruddick," an Oscar in her sight. It's the best script Jim and I have written. And the most personal. That's how we felt then, until another woman came into our life. Also with a name that started with "R."

6

ROSEANNE

While *we were working on "Ruthie's" many drafts,* we decided to pursue a regular TV gig again. We wanted to keep our momentum going in that world. Our agents suggested we write a spec of an existing show to reintroduce ourselves to the community. The problem was we didn't really like the sitcoms on at the time. The popular ones were mostly silly and joke-heavy, as opposed to character-driven comedies. There was one . . .

OCTOBER 8, 1992   JOURNAL ENTRY

The only sitcom we can stomach to write for is for *Roseanne,* so we've started one for that show. At first it was torture. Jim was not into it at all. I sat at the computer and just typed. It did teach me I could actually do it. If I only had the discipline to try something on my own. At this age I thought I'd have more answers. It's still all a bit confusing. I found a mantra to tell myself—TRUST THE RHYTHM OF LIFE!

I think one gets into trouble when you fight the natural flow. I hope the coming year is a fruit-ful one. I need to take steps to make sure that's possible. Create the best environment for healthy change.

Live in the moment

Be positive

Appreciate your accomplishments

Be open

Be loving

Care about others

Be receptive to new ideas

Expect Greatness

Stay healthy

Keep your sense of humor

Keeping journals over the years was therapy for me. I got to work through things, like how people think once you've been on a popular TV series, your life is perfect and that money keeps rolling in. It doesn't. Especially when you only work on a show for one season or you're not one of the main producers. Or creators. It was embarrassing having to sign up for unemployment, but I had to do it. I had house payments now. And I also didn't want to look like a loser to people in the business. Or to myself.

DECEMBER 31, 1992   JOURNAL ENTRY

I wish I could say it's been a good year. It has in some respects. Personal growth. But we have to get a job soon! Our *Roseanne* spec will hopefully jump-start our TV career. I want to remain optimistic. I was more depressed earlier this week. I guess the feeling of loneliness and not having someone romantic in my life. That would be so nice. Open arms. Open mind. Open heart. (How sappy is that?)

Luckily, our new agent, Paul Haas at ICM, really liked our *Roseanne* script. He was friendly with Melissa Gelineau, who worked for Jay Daniels at *Roseanne*. Jay was known as a "fixer" in the business. He was brought in to smooth things out between Roseanne and the creative team. The stories of the fights between Roseanne and the show's creator, Matt Williams, are legendary. By this point, Roseanne had banned Marcy Carsey and Tom Werner (aka Carsey-Werner), the producers, from the set. When does that ever happen?

Something else that doesn't normally happen is submitting a spec script you write for a show to that actual show. There's no way an outside writer can know the sound of the characters or the development of the storylines as well as the staff writers who are in the room every day. To our surprise, Jay and the showrunner, Rob Ulin, loved our spec *Roseanne* script. We met with them, and it seemed to go well. Although Rob and Jay said something really odd: "Don't expect any patting on the back. We don't do that here."

We said we didn't care about that. We probably would have said anything to get the job. We needed AND wanted it that bad. We had only one more hurdle: We had to meet Tom Arnold, Roseanne's husband (at the time), and get him to sign off on us. He was basically running things for her.

MAY 10, 1993   JOURNAL ENTRY

Tomorrow we go to Tom and Roseanne's house in Beverly Hills. Should be interesting. Everybody seems to be rooting for us. I guess if it's meant to be, it will. We're good writers that they could benefit from having us around.

To hedge our bets, Jim brought a crystal to the interview to surreptitiously leave somewhere in the cushion of one of their couches. But before he can do that, Tom comes barreling into the room.

He's not there five minutes when he says, "Let me ask you guys something. You gay?"

Without missing a beat, I said, "Is it the way we dress?"

We all laughed. My, how times have changed since we were called "Violets."

After the meeting, when we returned to Jim's car, we realized he had forgotten to leave the crystal behind. I made him go back and throw it over the wall of their vast compound, not even thinking they probably had security cameras all over the property.

MAY 17, 1993   JOURNAL ENTRY

We did it! We got the job!!!! Co-producers on *Roseanne*. We are SO happy. We also got two more offers from ABC. *Joe's Life* starring Peter Onorati by Bob Myer, and *Boy Meets World* by Michael Jacobs. Quite a week. Unemployed for exactly one year. I'm flying high, to say the least.

MAY 30, 1993   JOURNAL ENTRY

I'm real excited about going back on a show. It seems there are a lot of fun people on staff—Amy Sherman, Eric Gilliland, Betsy Borns (people have said great stuff about them). Lois Bromfield, we know. My life will change as of tomorrow. Who knows to what. Time will tell!

JUNE 1, 1993   JOURNAL ENTRY

Day One. A disaster? Not quite. Overwhelming? Absolutely! I was extremely quiet. And when I wasn't, I was very inarticulate. I haven't found my voice yet. It's like we've climbed aboard this fast-moving train. We've got our tickets but haven't taken our seats yet.

The first day was also when we got our first sighting of the force that is Amy Sherman. The "room" had been working on a "Darlene" storyline since we'd have to write all the Darlene/David scenes and shoot them early to accommodate Sara Gilbert's Yale schedule back East.

Then Amy whisks into the room. She's not seated but ten seconds and proceeds to rip apart the storyline and explain why it wouldn't make sense. I was blown away. All the writers' faces fell. They knew she was right but hated to be told that by a woman. Rob asked everyone to take a break. Jim and I immediately tracked Amy down in her office and told her what she said was spot on and impressive. We became fast friends. And learned quickly that Amy was not well-liked on the show. Respected, but not liked. I believe due to jealousy of her raw talent.

JUNE 22, 1993   JOURNAL ENTRY

Paul Haas said that Melissa Gelineau told him we were doing great at work. I feel like we're contributing a lot. Very pleasant and fun to be around. And still not at full speed. Just wait. Paul's gonna call Rob Ulin tomorrow and find out more. I want to stay there at least two years. I think I like almost everyone. Well, except two people. Not bad out of 21 writers. I wish Rob would feel more comfortable around us. Maybe it's the gay thing.

We did hear that Rob was confused about me and Jim. He asked in the writers' room, when we were in our office, why we weren't constantly having sex together since we were both gay. This from a guy who went to an Ivy League college. If he was thinking that, no wonder he was uncomfortable around us. I also got the sense that he (and the other writers) didn't like that Jim and I (and Lois Bromfield) became Amy Sherman's favorites.

Due to the large number of writers, Rob had us break into different rooms. Amy would request the three of us. If it was dinner time, she'd tell us to hop in her car, and we'd go to a nearby restaurant off the lot. I was always in a panic, fearing how the other writers would react if they found out we ordered a bottle of wine at dinner. Amy didn't care. She told me to relax. Well, she might have used a few swear words to get her point across. To Amy, all that mattered was that we came back with great scenes. And we did. Usually the Darlene/Roseanne bedroom scenes. Always my favorite.

Each writers' room at *Roseanne* had their own unique dynamic. In some rooms, I was really quiet. I think I was too intimidated. Like in Eric Gilliland's room. I did feel great and especially open in Miriam Trogdon or Steve Pepoon's room.

Often, Jim and I would be asked to head our own room. We usually got Roseanne and Tom's stand-up comic friends assigned to us. Those comedians would call it the "Tard Room." Finding that highly offensive, I begged them not to talk like that. Our rooms usually consisted of Lois (of course), Pat Bullard, Laura Kightlinger, Dave Raether, Mike Gandolfi, and Norm Macdonald. None of them had any sitcom writing experience. We had to teach them that their jokes, although completely hysterical, had to come from the character. I actually take pride that a bunch of them have gone on to successful TV writing careers. Norm would profess that he was going to be the Biggest Stand-Up Comedy Star Ever! He'd also invite me over to his house after work to smoke pot and get in his jacuzzi. I politely declined. He was married. But more importantly, I didn't really want to be in a hot tub naked with him. Although it would've made a good story for this book.

AUGUST 27, 1993   JOURNAL ENTRY

Work has been going much better. We're getting more positive feedback and feel much
more comfortable. If they didn't ask us back,
they would be crazy. We're making a major

contribution to the show. I can't wait until
the season premiere in three weeks. Plus, the
new opening credit sequence around the kitchen
table is our idea. The Conners eating Chinese
food. I do hate at work when talk leads to
everyone and their wives or lovers. It makes
me feel lonely and like a total failure.

The series was known for its high turnover rate. Early on, we heard
from writers who had lasted on the show how to survive Roseanne's
firings. They advised us to find the tallest person on set and stand
behind them. If Roseanne couldn't see the whites of your eyes, she
couldn't fire you.

The first day of rehearsal, Roseanne and Tom, with a gleam in *their*
eyes, told all of the writers to stand in line; they had made T-shirts for
us. Numbered T-shirts. Since my birthday is October 13, I counted
and stood in line to get No. 13.

As we were waiting, the mood of the staff turned. Word trickled
out why they had numbered the shirts—so that Tom & Roseanne
wouldn't have to learn our names and could just point and say, "Number
13, you're fired!" Tom and Roseanne thought this was hysterical. At the
time, it didn't really sink in how degrading that was. I was just glad I
had my birth date on my shirt. I still have that shirt and cherish it.

SEPTEMBER 12, 1993   JOURNAL ENTRY

Last night, Roseanne finally won an Emmy. Today
she doesn't show up to the table reading. I
thought this would be an easy week. Nope. She
was holed up in her trailer, refusing to come
out. But during the reading, we all see her
enter on the side of the set. Standing in a
long white t-shirt. Barefoot, holding shoes.
Tom runs over to her and pulls her behind the
set, and we hear muffled yelling. Cut to 9:30

```
p.m. Jim, Lois, Amy, and I return from a work/
dinner to learn that Roseanne will go to the
Friar's Roast tomorrow, film this week's epi-
sode, then go to a sanitarium for two weeks'
rest. We will film one episode without her.
Rob Ulin had to drive to their house with Jay
Daniel for this information. I feel sad for
her. I'm not totally surprised, though. She
seems so unhappy.
```

That was the week Roseanne went off to get electric shock treatments. Up until that day, I didn't know they still did that. I thought it was something done to old Hollywood movie stars, like Frances Farmer. But as Roseanne has publicly stated, and written books about, she's dealt with mental health issues and having multiple personalities. I was under the crazy assumption that if I could simply hug her and let her know that people cared, everything would be alright. When the other writers heard me say that, they thought I was the one who needed electric shock.

So, without Roseanne in a show called *Roseanne*, we had to create an entirely new episode. This was especially difficult since we'd been trained to have Roseanne's character drive every scene. And suddenly there was no Roseanne. We were sent off to a room to pitch on possible storylines. We liked using information from past episodes and came up with a show about an old girlfriend of Dan's. Here's a description of that episode:

*Dan and Roseanne get an invitation to their fifteenth high school class reunion. While looking over some old photographs to bring for the yearbook, Roseanne finds out that Dan had a fling with another girl a long time ago. It was a one-night stand, but it was with Roseanne's high school nemesis. The girl turns out to be Phyllis Zimmer, played by Vicki Lawrence (*The Carol Burnett Show*).*

My favorite part of working on the show was coming up with the tags. Tags are an extra little piece of the show that doesn't have much story in it. They do that in case they want to cut it from airing during syndication, leaving more time to sell commercials. On *Roseanne*, we prided ourselves on creating really way-out tags. For that episode, I thought it would be fun to have Vicki Lawrence try to explain the lyrics to her one-hit single, "The Night the Lights Went Out in Georgia," a record I had as a kid. I pitched the idea of having Vicki with a diagram on a chalkboard. Rob liked it, and it was filmed. Talk about a full-circle moment.

NOVEMBER 4, 1993   JOURNAL ENTRY

Tomorrow they read our script ("The Driver's Seat") at the table. Nerve-racking. Tom had no notes. Oh, we got our option for the second part of the season picked up. Which means, it's the longest staff job we've ever had. I don't know if I want to come back next year. It's very hard work, and at times I don't feel up to it. But other times are real highs. Let's hope this week is one of them.

While working on *Roseanne*, I got to touch Brett Butler's breasts. Yes, you read that correctly.

To save money, producers Carsey-Werner set up a kitchen to feed all the writers on their many sitcoms in production. It also saves time from having to figure out food orders and sending PAs out to pick up our meals.

So, one day, as I'm waiting in line to fill my plate, Brett, whose show *Grace Under Fire* was another big hit for ABC, announces to some of the guys in line that she recently got her boobs done. And they're real hard.

She looks at me and says, "Go ahead and touch 'em!"

I hesitated, thinking she was joking. She wasn't. Then she grabs my free hand and places it on one of her breasts. And there I was, touching a woman's breast for the first time since Rande's in her parents' den in Oceanside, Long Island. They were indeed hard. (Don't worry; that's the only thing that was.)

I complimented her on the shape and firmness, grabbed my silverware and napkin, and flew out the door. Nowadays, production companies are sued for that kind of sexual impropriety, but back then, disturbing as it may have been, the behavior was usually laughed off. You didn't want to make waves and lose your job.

NOVEMBER 15, 1993   JOURNAL ENTRY

The reading of our episode went great. Roseanne seemed to laugh a bit at a lot of the jokes. She also loved the drama of it and how we handled her character hitting DJ, when he took the family car out for a joy ride. But she was completely horrible to Rob and called the staff, "Twenty-one motherfuckers." Lovely. On tape night she gave the most incredible performance I have ever seen from her. If she doesn't win another Emmy, I'd be shocked. Let's just hope we're there with her and visualize all the prizes going to us—Emmy, WGA Award, Golden Globe, etc.!

Tape nights on *Roseanne* were unlike any show we worked on. First, they had changed a bit from our days on *The Golden Girls*. Now the executive producers would be on the floor, the stage where the sets, actors, and cameras are. The writing staff was in a booth, way up behind the bleachers. We weren't allowed on stage until after the show wrapped. Filming would typically go fast on *Roseanne*. She liked to do one take of a scene and then move on. Maybe film a "pickup" shot or two. She wanted the show to feel like it just happened. Not rehearsed and too polished. You have to give her credit. She knew what she wanted. It's too bad she created such a toxic work environment to get it. It would have been so much nicer if she had replaced all the people she complained about and brought love and respect to the workplace. She had everyone working from a place of fear.

The actors rarely talked to the writers when we came down to the stage to watch the afternoon run-throughs. I didn't know that in the beginning. So, I marched right over to Laurie Metcalf to tell her I was a huge fan of her performance in Chicago's famed Steppenwolf Theatre Company's production of Lanford Wilson's play *Balm in Gilead*. I took Jim and other friends to see its very successful run at Circle Rep in Greenwich Village. Laurie had this four-page monologue. I sat in awe, never having witnessed such a raw and dynamic actor like that up close. I suggested to her that someone should film that production to have it for posterity. She just grinned back at me and didn't engage in any dialogue. I later learned that she was afraid of losing her job if she was seen talking with a writer. Rumor was that Lecy Goranson, the "original" Becky, was replaced by Sarah Chalke on our year because Lecy started dating a crew member. Speaking of Sarah Chalke, she was like a deer in the headlights when she first arrived on that show. Sweet, but always uncomfortable in that role and with doing multi-cam comedy. It's been great to see her grow as an actor and really find her comedy chops.

So, I learned to keep my distance from the actors whenever we went down to the floor. Which made it odd when Sandra would be there for her episodes. She was my friend, and I wanted to gab with her. I also didn't understand why the writers in the room seemed hesitant to give her character, "Nancy," good lines or strong stories. Were they intimidated? Not sure how to write for her since they were all straight? I thought it was a missed opportunity. Since getting to know her, I had gone to a lot of her live shows. She has such sharp comic timing. What aren't they getting about her?

I suggested Jim, Rob Ulin, and I take her to lunch to discuss her character and possible new storylines she might like to play. She shrugged off the offer. I didn't understand why she would so easily pass up the opportunity. Looking back now, I think she was grateful for the gig and didn't want to get on Roseanne's bad side. Roseanne perceived the writers as the enemy. It's amazing we were all able to produce such a creatively inspiring show amongst such negativity and chaos. I think our season was probably one of the strongest during the entire original series. We got to deal with some amazing issues in a funny and honest way. This was exactly the style of writing we loved and had been yearning to do. But as in any job, office politics often comes into play. Especially with such a dysfunctional boss at the helm. You tend to second guess everything.

December 20, 1993: *Paranoia has set in since Rob has been excluding us from the big room, late nights, and even Sundays. We've been given lots to do, scene wise. A lot of our material stays in. It's strange. We have no sense of how we're doing. I'm proud of all the work Jim and I have done. But we get no credit and no acknowledgment. They warned us about that. But now we start thinking about next season. I don't know if I want to come back. More than Jim, though. Since our options were picked up for the second half of the season, I've really loosened up. Getting many more jokes in. It feels good.*

January 31, 1994: *What a week! They assigned the lesbian kiss episode to us. And hired us to rewrite a Sandra Bernhard pilot. We went from the back of the bus to the front of the parade. Very exciting. To finally have our work acknowledged. Supposedly Roseanne read the script and was laughing out loud. She said this was the fucking funniest script this season!*

We were fortunate to be able to write the infamous "Lesbian Kiss" episode of *Roseanne*. That storyline came about because we used what we had learned from Rue on *Golden Girls*. Challenge the main character. We wondered, if Roseanne was so liberal (at that time!), what would make her and her family freak out a little? What if she was kissed by a woman at a gay bar? We had no idea what HUGE drama that would cause. At work. At the network. In the world. It was so odd to go to the studio lot during the day and write it, then come home at night and hear them talking about your episode on the eleven o'clock news or nighttime talk shows.

FEBRUARY 12, 1994   JOURNAL ENTRY

The controversy over the kiss episode is wild. All over the papers, *David Letterman*, *Hard Copy*, etc. I hope ABC will air it. We're planning a big viewing party as a benefit for GLAAD. Also, Tom picked up our option for next year, with a bump to supervising producers. That is so cool.

FEBRUARY 27, 1994   JOURNAL ENTRY

What a week! I say that every week. But the coming one is even more eventful. Tuesday night is the airing of the big kiss episode. We're expecting over two hundred people for our GLAAD viewing party. I have no idea how the evening will turn out, but it's all so exciting.

The benefit/screening at Studio One was my first real taste of the power of mass media. Tons of entertainment outlets covered it. And they wanted to talk to *us*. We'd come a long way from being in the closet at work, and I wasn't about to shy away from grabbing this moment. For all those LGBTQ kids out there to see that you could be your authentic self and still succeed. It didn't mean there wouldn't be struggles. Obviously, there were to even get this episode on the air. And God bless Tom and Roseanne. They threatened ABC that they'd buy the episode back and air it on HBO if the network wouldn't. ABC agreed, and the rest is history.

MARCH 5, 1994   JOURNAL ENTRY

So intense. At our benefit for GLAAD for the kiss episode, close to five hundred people were in attendance! We raised about $5,000. We did interviews with *CNN* and *E!* and *Entertainment Weekly*. It truly was a historic event. Next stop, hopefully the Emmys!

It was an electrifying moment, to be standing there amongst so many people, lots of friends, and worldwide media, when Mariel Hemingway kissed Roseanne on the big screen. We didn't know what the final network edit would be. But when it happened, the packed room erupted in cheers. Chills went down my spine.

There is *one* moment of the show that I don't care for. I don't like that Roseanne wipes her mouth on her sleeve after the kiss. It was Roseanne's idea and done for comic effect. I think it's totally unnecessary and takes away from the power of the moment. I let Rob Ulin know how I felt, as I was starting to be a little more opinionated at work. But I was merely a writer on the show, and he thought it was funny. Most of the writers did too. I didn't mind having an unpopular opinion. Or being called too sensitive. One of the most important lessons I've learned in this business is to PICK YOUR BATTLES. We won the big one by getting that kiss on network television. It was a huge ratings winner. No sponsors backed away from the show. And the world didn't explode.

There was so much craziness during that year on *Roseanne*. She (and Tom) seemed to thrive in that chaotic space. A biggie was when we were off the Radford lot helping Amy Sherman with her *Cherry Street, South of Main* pilot she wrote for Tom and Roseanne's production company. It was created as a vehicle for the female singing group, En Vogue. But then the network (ABC) found out that the four singers were not actors. Or funny. So, they had to totally recast. One who we found out during run-throughs was also not funny. Or was at least not multi-cam comedy funny. Which is a whole separate talent. That was Salma Hayek. Try to find information on that ill-fated pilot online. You can't.

Things blew up the day before filming. Roseanne claimed that Tom was sleeping with Kim Silva, their assistant/development executive. We'd gotten pretty close with Kim while rewriting the Sandra Bernhard pilot. First Roseanne goes nuts with the news. Then she publicly says they're going to enter into a three-way marriage. Probably to save face. That caused the media to go even nuttier. But then Roseanne's friends, who never liked Tom, talked her into kicking him out of their Beverly Hills house. He moved into an expensive penthouse in a high-rise on Wilshire Boulevard. Jim and I were summoned over there to pull an all-nighter and rewrite the Sandra script with Tom. He was probably lonely and wanted company. They eventually got divorced, and anyone who Roseanne perceived to be on Tom's side was the enemy.

MAY 4, 1994   JOURNAL ENTRY

Well, it finally happened. I had a feeling. Rob Ulin did not ask us back to *Roseanne*. Which is odd, since Tom had already talked to our agent about bumping us up to a higher title next year. I want to sue. Jim doesn't. I'm feeling so many things. It wasn't a healthy environment. But now we have to get another job. What the hell will it be? I know it's better in the long run. It's the short run that I'm worried about. And how do we look in the eyes of the industry? I know it will sort itself out. I also have to tell our friends. It's hard to keep this a secret.

I'm really glad we had that job in the first place. We got to move the needle. I don't know if *Ellen* or *Will & Grace* would have happened so soon after without our episode. Kids today may not understand what the big deal was. But it was. I'm grateful for all I learned on the show, all I taught the newbie writers, and the relationships that were formed. So much has come from that experience.

Years later, I'd rack up another full-circle moment, this time with the *Roseanne* show. Wendy Baxter at Sony International would occasionally check my availability to drop everything and travel overseas for an extended period of time to be a writing consultant. I always said yes, but nothing ever came of it. Until the beginning of 2015. This time she was serious. But it was only for a two-to-three-month gig, maybe longer, in Moscow. To help them develop a Russian *Roseanne* show. Since Jim and I didn't have a paying gig at the time, I had no choice but to seriously entertain the offer. Also, Wendy kind of dangled a few more exotic locations where I could possibly work if this gig went well.

A bunch of my friends were extremely skeptical. Especially Michael Urie, who told me about some gay guy getting a pole shoved up his ass over there. I'd heard frightening stories of gangs in Moscow that targeted gay guys. They'd get them to come over for a date, then jump them and film them being brutalized. I went straight to my computer and traumatized myself even more with all the horrific videos and stories that popped up. But I needed the money, so I said "yes" to Russia. Even though I secretly hoped that Jim and I would land a job before I had to leave in the spring.

The world had other plans for me. And so, with barely a few weeks' notice, I signed a two-month agreement to go. With an option for a third month. One of the articles I read stated that even mentioning anything gay in Russia was considered a crime. I had to ask Wendy what if an executive or writer over there asked about my lesbian kiss episode? And what would happen if there was suddenly some political situation between our two countries? She tried to calm my nerves, saying they wanted to concentrate on the first few seasons of *Roseanne*, when there wasn't really mention of anything gay. Okay . . . and she also told me that they recently hired a security firm that could whisk

me out of the country in the middle of the night if anything bad started to happen.

I joked, "You mean, like I'm in some Tom Cruise adventure movie?"
"Yes," she said.

I guess it wasn't a joke.

So, Thursday, April 16, passport in hand, I boarded Aeroflot Flight
0107 to Moscow. The minute I stepped on the plane, I breathed into
the adventure. I especially loved the female flight attendants' 1950s
Mad Men retro uniforms and gloves. And I was put in first class.
Champagne was immediately poured. Maybe this wouldn't be so bad
after all.

It was a long flight, so I timed out when I would take my sleeping
pill and put on my comfy eye shades. Next thing I knew, we were
landing at Domodedovo Airport. I was met by my driver and translator and taken to my apartment on Tverskaya Street. Sitting by the
elevator, checking everyone in, was the meanest looking woman I'd
ever seen. That is, until the next day, when she was replaced by an even
meaner looking woman.

My apartment was big, and I was excited to get settled. But I didn't
have time; they wanted me to meet with Jeff Lerner, head of Sony
International, who was in town for a day from LA. So back in my
black BMW I went, and my driver took me through horrible Moscow
traffic to a fancy hotel, where I immediately ordered a triple espresso
to help me get through jet lag.

Jeff was great, and I told him I was ready to go to any and all
comedy clubs to find the Russian "Roseanne." The way Roseanne Barr
was found doing stand-up. One problem: Comedy clubs don't exist in
Russia. We'd have to read actors. But first I had to help them pick a
director. They had set up a bunch of meetings with possible candidates
I'd have to choose from.

ME? I thought I was merely consulting. Nope. I'd be working with
a new writer, but they loved having me there since I'd been a showrunner and had an extensive background in theater and casting with

Leonard Finger in college.

I really wanted to hire a woman, but the one female director candidate gave an awful interview. The minute she sat down, she started telling me how the original *Roseanne* wasn't funny, and this new script wasn't very good. I explained that the charm of the show was that it mixed real life with humor and pathos. This was all communicated through my translator. She wasn't buying it. I guess they interview differently in Russia.

Next!

I landed on one of the biggest comedy theater directors in Russia, and we got along famously. We agreed about ninety-eight percent of the time on actors we both liked. It was so interesting; even though I didn't understand a word of Russian, I could tell if the actors were funny.

Unfortunately, the network had a hard time watching the audition tapes. They didn't understand why the actors were in an office building and not in Katya's (the name they changed "Roseanne" to) kitchen. Frustrated, I went back home to the United States after two months. They wanted me to stay for a third, but I was ready for the comforts of home. And I wanted to present an original play at the 2015 Hollywood Fringe Festival. My first time writing solo.

Back in LA, I had a brainstorm. Since they were still filming Phil Rosenthal's Russian version of his popular hit, *Everybody Loves Raymond*, now called *The Voronins*, I thought, *Why don't we shoot the screen tests on their kitchen set? Just move the refrigerator around and change up the table and props.* Everyone loved my idea.

Upon my return in the fall of 2015 for another two-month stint abroad, I was able to talk the famous Russian singer, Lolita Milyavskaya, into testing for us. She was a controversial figure, being that she was outspoken about gay and women's rights. Being outspoken about anything was unheard of there. But it seemed so right to me for the essence of *Roseanne*.

While I was there on my second tour of duty, I also helped develop a Russian *Mary Tyler Moore Show*. For that, I was successful in getting them to hire a woman to write the pilot. But then the producers insisted on also adding on a male joke writer to "make it funny." They have a bit of a ways to go in that country as far as equal rights go.

I had an amazing time there and feel so fortunate to have had that once in a lifetime experience. And I'm forever grateful that my second apartment was so close to Red Square that I could see it from my balcony. I made some great friendships with the other American writers who were there at the same time as me. I even dated. I learned early on to never have a guy come to your apartment. Always meet by a monument. And since I couldn't pronounce any of the statues' names, I would refer to them by how they looked. So, it would be, "Meet me by the soldier with sword sitting on the horse," or something like that. And I have Roseanne Barr-Pentland-Arnold-Thomas-Barr to thank for that.

My dealings with Roseanne didn't end in Russia. On the morning of May 29, 2018, I turned on my computer and phone, as I tend to do when I wake up and am still in bed. Facebook was going nuts with posts about how Roseanne had tweeted: *muslim brotherhood & planet of the apes had a baby=vj.*

Roseanne was supposedly referring to President Obama's senior advisor, Valerie Jarrett. She later said she thought Valerie was white. Next, I see a post from Wanda Sykes, the brilliant comic and writer on the *Roseanne* reboot. Wanda says she's quitting the show because of that racist tweet. Things moved quickly. Faster than I had ever seen in this town. Suddenly ABC Entertainment President Channing Dungey issued this statement: "Roseanne's Twitter statement is abhorrent, repugnant, and inconsistent with our values, and we have decided to cancel her show."

Just like that, the reboot show was history. Even though it had been ABC's highest rated and most watched new series. I was surprised the network would give up on such a big money maker. I guess they were tired of Roseanne's antics and didn't want to deal with her anymore. It didn't help that even Sara Gilbert, a costar and producer on the show, was speaking out against what Roseanne had done.

Someone I kind of knew, Bill Hinkle, Brooke Baldwin's producer, messaged me and asked if I'd go live on Brooke's "CNN Newsroom" show in a couple hours to talk about it. I immediately called my friend, Peter Golden. I expected him to tell me to not to do it, but he said the opposite. So, I texted Bill back and agreed to appear. I hopped in the shower. They were sending a car to take me to CNN studios in Hollywood in an hour. As I washed my hair, I went over my thoughts. I didn't want to sound stupid on live TV. But I had a definite take on the events of the morning.

An hour later, a big, black SUV with tinted windows pulled up to my house. I jumped in, wearing my No. 13 *Roseanne* T-shirt, and since the studio is merely ten minutes away, before I knew it, we arrived. I'm whisked into hair and makeup. Then, as I attempt to gulp down some more coffee, I'm put in a small, dark room in front of two monitors and a fake LA skyline flat behind me.

The cameraman comes in and asks, "You wanna wear an earpiece? But I gotta warn ya, you'll have a second or two delay."

Me: "I've never done anything like this. What do most people do?"

He says, "They take the earpiece."

With time running out until we're live on the air, I say, "I'll take the earpiece!"

He helps me put in the earpiece properly, then disappears. I thought he'd be in the room with me.

Suddenly, I could hear Brooke doing her show in New York. Then she closes her segment with a tease about me coming up. Me! I could've gotten nervous, but I decided to do what I tell my acting students: *Be present and talk from the heart.*

The commercial break winds down, then I hear a countdown from the Control Room, "You're live in five, four, three, two . . ."

I then see my image pop up on screen with Brooke's, and her mouth is moving, but it's not in sync due to the delay.

Brooke: "My next guest had a seat at the *Roseanne* show's writers' table during its first, incredibly successful run in the 90s. He worked directly with Roseanne Barr. He is Stan Zimmerman . . ."

And we're off and running.

Brooke couldn't have been nicer, but like any good reporter, she wanted a scoop. I stuck to my agenda. I made sure to talk about how conflicted I was since Roseanne had been such a champion for the underdog during my days on the show, especially for my lesbian kiss episode. I was as surprised as everyone else about her recent change in politics to become a Trumper. I took the position that Roseanne should not have been fired from her own show, and the series should have remained on the air. Although I don't approve of what she said, I felt it could be a teachable moment. I wish Roseanne had taken responsibility for her hurtful words and challenged herself to learn and be better. I believe one of the reasons we're so polarized in America is because we push people away instead of keeping them around to have some difficult and messy discussions.

And then the interview was over. I was whisked back into my waiting SUV. I'm catching my breath when suddenly my cell rings: It's ABC News. They saw me on CNN and wanted to book me to film an interview about Roseanne to air on a number of their programs—*Good Morning, America*; *ABC Evening News*; *Nightline*; etc. It was extremely exciting. A bunch of random people start sending me pictures they took when they were at the gym or home and by chance caught my appearance.

But that's not the end of the story for Roseanne.

On May 29, 2018, she tweeted: *I apologize to Valerie Jarrett and to all Americans. I am truly sorry for making a bad joke about her politics and her looks. I should have known better. Forgive me—my joke was in bad taste.* Later, she added, *I am now leaving Twitter.*

But does she let that go? Oh, no. Not Roseanne. A day later, she's blaming her initial comments on being under the influence of the sleeping pill, Ambien. I love that the company that makes

Ambien responds with this quote: "Racism is not a known side effect." Somebody there is a witty writer.

And in true Roseanne fashion, she makes matters worse. She starts ragging on Sara Gilbert and all liberals. Such a wasted opportunity to get her show back, educate herself, and possibly even move society a bit. Or at least provoke much-needed discussion. Especially in the format of such groundbreaking television. Her show was a far cry from the fake, wholesome family sitcoms I grew up with.

THE BRADY LADIES

Before *ABC-TV came up with their famous* "TGIF" (Thank God It's Friday) tag line, they had a legendary lineup of Friday shows. I was glued to our Zenith TV, starting at eight p.m. with *The Brady Bunch,* then *The Partridge Family, Room 222, The Odd Couple,* and ending with *Love, American Style* at ten p.m.

Sitting on our brown Naugahyde couch in our den, I had no idea one day I would be offered the opportunity to rewrite a movie based on *The Brady Bunch.* But that's exactly what happened in April 1994 when our film agent, Richard Feldman, called.

Richard: "Hey, are you two interested in doing a production polish on a movie at Paramount?"

We didn't have to hear more to say, "Yes!"

He told us to read the latest draft and see if it was something up our alley. I knew it would be and was even more excited when I was told his client, Betty Thomas, an Emmy winner for her role as "Lucy Bates" on NBC's hit ensemble cop show, *Hill Street Blues,* would be directing.

I was literally packing my bags for a vacation to Greece (Athens, Mykonos, and then finally the magical island of Santorini) when the script arrived at my door. I read it instantly. To be honest, I didn't find it that funny. It had a clever premise—The Brady family (and their trusted maid, Alice) were stuck in the 1970s even though they lived in current day, 1985. They were still the wholesome, dorky, polyester-clad characters I grew up with. But I felt there were so many joke areas left untapped in the current draft. And there were a lot of writers' names on it. About four teams. And that didn't include the Schwartzes, even though Sherwood Schwartz created the series. Or Joey and Faith Soloway, who created *The Real Live Brady Bunch*, a cult hit stage show in 1991. It had super successful runs in Chicago, New York, and eventually LA. The format for this parody play was a word-for-word reenactment of one of the episodes for Act One. And a Brady-based game show for Act Two. It was pretty hysterical and really campy. Jim and I went to see it at the Westwood Playhouse. Jane Lynch (pre-*Glee*) played Carol Brady, and Andy Richter (pre-*Conan O'Brien Show*) was Mike Brady. Bonnie and Terry Turner (*Third Rock from the Sun*) did a major rewrite on the film script, and I believe were the ones who came up with the concept of the movie.

We told our agent we were very interested. We desperately wanted to work on a movie that was actually being filmed, not just in development. But I wasn't willing to cancel my trip, so off to Greece I went.

After a harrowing cab ride from the Athens airport to my hotel, I wanted to hide in my room. Then the phone rang. It was a low voice. No "hello," just, "You wanna come back and write *The Brady Bunch Movie* for me?!" I thought it was a man. It was Betty Thomas. She had recently had a meeting with Jim. He told her I was a Brady expert. Small lie. I know a lot about them but would never consider myself an expert.

I said, "Give me the weekend in Mykonos, and then I'm all yours." I immediately changed my plans, skipping the Santorini portion of my trip.

Our first day on the job at producer Alan Ladd's offices on the Paramount lot, Betty said to think of writing it for three different types of audiences:

1) Brady fans that grew up with the show
2) Kids that had never watched the show
3) Stoners

We were all in! She showed us to our office. It was so tiny, you couldn't even call it a room. Yep, we were back in the closet! But this time, we were out and gay and bringing that POV to the table. Because most of the scenes and locations had already been scouted, Betty gave us carte blanche to rewrite any dialogue within a scene. Nothing was too crazy or off limits.

Periodically during the day, Betty would come in to check on us. It felt so great to make her laugh so hard she'd fall on the floor. Literally. I have photographic proof. We all really clicked as far as our senses of humor.

After our two weeks were up, the studio extended our contract for another two. Then another two. That kept going all summer. So, thank you, Bradys, for helping to pay my mortgage.

Betty would often ask our advice on actors she was meeting. Since my background was in casting, I would come to work with lists of actor names. I suggested some famous ones for the role of "Alice," like Rosie O'Donnell and Kathy Najimy. But Betty didn't care about stars. She wanted the best actors for the roles. Actors that would get the tone of what we were doing. It was a fine line we were asking them to maneuver. Be real, but slightly heightened. And they had to "get the joke."

One day, Betty came into our closet/office and had us listen to the taped audition for the part of "Mike Brady."

Betty: "Shut your eyes and try and guess who the actor is."

It was uncanny how similar he sounded to Robert Reed. We couldn't figure out who it was. It didn't help that this actor was not known for comedy. And he wasn't even a movie actor.

Finally, Betty blurted out: "It's Gary Cole! From *Midnight Caller*, an NBC drama series. Hardly a household name or movie star. But we all agreed she had to cast him.

Now that we had our Mike Brady, we needed to find the other half of the most famous TV couple—Carol Brady. Betty met with lots of actors but really liked her old friend and costar from "*Troop Beverly Hills*," Shelley Long. Jim and I loved the idea since we were huge fans of *Cheers*, the script that put us on the map. Shelley seemed slightly older than Gary Cole, but she was so friggin' funny, and people knew her. But Shelley wasn't considered a movie star anymore and had a reputation for being difficult on her last few movie sets.

Betty believed in Shelley but wanted to make sure she was comfortable with everything. Betty asked us to come into her office when she had that heart-to-heart call with Shelley. I'm not sure why, but Jim and I wound up sitting under Betty's desk as she talked to her on speakerphone. She made us promise not to make a peep.

Betty: "Shel, you gotta be cool with this being an ensemble movie. It's not a Shelley Long vehicle."

Shelley was cool with it, loved the material, and wanted to work with Betty. A deal was set. What impressed me most about Shelley was that I heard she came in on her days off to read with the other actors during their close-up shots. When she wasn't on camera. I think she was making a conscious effort to prove to the industry that she could be a team player. Who knows if the stories were true, and she was trouble on other sets; or was it simply the times, and women weren't supposed to ask for too much on the job? Either way, she had a brilliant take on Carol/Florence Henderson. She played it with exactly the right wink to the audience.

But in my opinion, two new actors stole the film—Christine Taylor and Jennifer Elise Cox as "Marcia" and "Jan." Christine had played a lead in the Nickelodeon kids' show, *Hey Dude*. Jennifer's last job was as an ice cream scooper at a Ben & Jerry's store in Gramercy Park. And get this: The store's owner was none other than my Uncle Jerry, my mom's older brother. What are the odds?!

Once we saw what those two gifted comediennes were capable of in dailies (footage shot from the day before), we knew we had to write more material for them. We decided to go even further with their intense sibling rivalry. Those two actors took their characters to a whole new level. Christine also had the good fortune of being a dead ringer for Maureen McCormick, the original "Marcia Brady" from the

70s TV series. And the way she pronounced "school" as "skeewl" was other worldly.

I'm taking full credit for getting RuPaul cast in the movie. Now we all know Ru from his wildly popular show, *RuPaul's Drag Race.* Back then, he was a struggling drag queen in the LGBTQ nightclub scene in Manhattan. I was nursing a vodka martini one night at the Revolver Video Bar in West Hollywood, and all of a sudden, an eye-popping music video for a new dance song called "Supermodel (You Better Work)" came up on all the big screens in the bar. Everyone was mesmerized by this gorgeous, tall, Black, drag artist named RuPaul. Maybe it was the liquor talking, but I had a lightbulb moment. What if he played Ms. Cummings, Jan's wise school guidance counselor?

The next morning, I ran into work all abuzz. I couldn't wait to tell Betty my crazy idea. We had been reading brilliant, Black actresses for the part, like my ol' pal Jenifer Lewis, but no one seemed right. Betty laughed hard and had Deb Aquila, our casting director, track Ru down. He got the part!

I knew I had to go to the filming of his first scene with Jan.

After a few takes, I leaned over and whispered to Betty: "At the end, before Jan exits, can you have Ru say, "And girl, you better work!"

Betty looked at me quizzically.

I said, "Trust me. Just for one take."

Betty shrugged and went onto the set and whispered to Ru to say that. Thank God, we got that in the can because by the time the movie opened, that song was huge! Betty even punctuated the scene with music from the song.

SEPTEMBER 18, 1994   JOURNAL ENTRY

The Brady Bunch Movie wrapped. The studio seems pretty happy. They had a cool wrap party. This great psychic woman told me how much success I'm about to have. Fingers crossed . . .

NOVEMBER 15, 1994   JOURNAL ENTRY

Bad news. We just learned we're not getting
screen credit on *The Brady Bunch Movie*. We
were VERY upset when we found out. But our
agents told us that everyone in town knows
that we rewrote it. Which is great since we've
seen a recent cut and think it's going to be a
big hit. Word on it is already great.

FEBRUARY 19, 1995   JOURNAL ENTRY

Brady Movie opened. $3.5 million in one day.
So much to tell about opening night driving around in a limo with Betty, Jenno, Jim,
and our agent. Stopping at different theaters
in LA. By the time we got to the late show
at Universal City, kids were sitting in the
aisle. I can't even put into words how exciting it is. I only wish our names were on it.
Oh, well!

But the industry knew we were responsible for the tone and most
of the jokes in the movie. And due to the overwhelming success of
that movie, Paramount ordered a sequel. Betty didn't want to direct
it, so they hired another woman who had directed the HBO show
Dream On, Arlene Sanford. This would be Arlene's feature film debut.
She was a lesbian, so of course we got along instantly. But Arlene's
personality is completely different from Betty's. Betty is assertive and
opinionated. Arlene is much quieter and more inward. A thinker. And
she looked to us for how we did the first movie.

Before we even opened our computer, I said that RuPaul had to be
in the sequel. Arlene wondered how since the movie took place during
the summer. They wouldn't be shooting any scenes at school.

I immediately pitched, "What if Ms. Cummings was at the

Community Pool scene?"

Arlene: "Why would she be there?"

Without missing a beat, I said, "She's with her three Black daughters. One that complained about her older, attention-grabbing sister, 'Moesha, Moesha, Moesha!'"

Arlene and Jim laughed hard, and that joke stayed in.

Because of the cult status of the first film, actors sought us out to do a cameo, like Rosie O'Donnell. But she'd only do it if we'd write something for her and her pal Zsa Zsa Gabor to do together. Jim and I were asked if we could speak with Zsa Zsa on the phone one Sunday. Having watched her and her sister Eva on many TV shows, we said, "Of course." I was so excited when I heard her famous Hungarian accent on the phone. She was cool with us, even making a joke about being arrested for slapping a Beverly Hills cop on the face during a routine traffic stop. She was such a good sport.

We were grateful for the opportunity to create the sequel from the beginning. And especially to get the chance to go even wilder with the Brady clan. But then we had a major decision to make.

In February of 1995, FOX network agreed to make our pilot, *Road Warriors*. Our very first one! We didn't know what to do. After trying to work on both projects at the same time, we felt we wouldn't be giving either the full attention they needed. Since both were for Paramount, we asked the studio to let us go make the pilot and then come back onto *Brady* once our pilot was cast and shot. They agreed and hired a writing team to work on a few drafts in our absence.

Road Warriors was a half-hour ensemble comedy about traveling salespeople. This was way before the George Clooney movie, *Up in the Air*. We saw it as a cross between *Cheers* and the David Mamet play, *Glengarry Glen Ross*. Our showrunners were Mort Nathan & Barry Fanaro from *The Golden Girls*. They had an overall deal at Paramount, and we got to talking to them through the window of our office/closet on *Brady*. It was great to be working with them after so many years. Especially since now we didn't have to hide who we were. They said they knew the whole time we were on *Golden Girls.*

Once that cat was out of the bag, we found they wanted to talk about gay stuff ALL the time. When a beautiful woman would walk by the office window at Paramount, one of them would turn to us and say, "Nothing?"

We shook our heads, "Nope." That didn't do it for us.

It felt great to finally feel free enough to reciprocate the joke. When a hot guy would walk by, we'd turn to them and say, "Nothing?"

Since this was our first pilot, everything seemed new and exciting. Especially auditioning actors during casting.

We had to go the Van Nuys Airport and meet Sean Astin to talk him into doing a multi-cam comedy. Our charm worked. But finding the "Diane" to his "Sam" was not easy. We saw so many up-and-coming young actresses. We narrowed it down to three to take to the network—Mariska Hargitay (now of *Law and Order*), Elaine Hendrix (went on to star in *The Parent Trap*), and Jamie Luner (*Just the Ten of Us*). Elaine got the part and was brilliant. Smart, sexy, with such a dry sense of humor. Not surprising that she has worked continuously. I only wish it were with me again!

MAY 1, 1995   JOURNAL ENTRY

Filming of our pilot went great. My mom was at the first taping. Sitting in the front row, in the "Queen's seat," as she liked to call it. It seems like a show that Fox needs and will pick up. Who knows. It's out of our hands now.

Sadly, the network passed. It crushed us. The show was so sharp and funny and something I've never seen before on network TV. Luckily, we had *A Very Brady Sequel* to keep us occupied. We took back the script and started in on rewrites. But this time there seemed to be much more at stake for the studio, and they had their hands all over the script. And with that came drama.

DECEMBER 10, 1995   JOURNAL ENTRY

I find out that Paramount asked my good friend
Elaine to rewrite *Brady 2*. I was very upset.
Lost sleep. I can be too sensitive. But I
handled the next week well. I told our agent,
Richard; he yelled at Tom Levine (the Paramount
exec), and I was able to tell Arlene my feelings without being too emotional. The story
gets better. We do Ladd Company and Arlene's
notes all week. On Thursday, the studio green-
lights the script. There are messengers camped
out in front of our houses with gift baskets.
Bottom line, everyone flipped over the script.
We're heroes. Even Tom Levine called us and
said we "hit it out of the park." Very gratifying! I just wish I hadn't got so emotional
in the beginning.

JUNE 14, 1996   JOURNAL ENTRY

Just found out our names will finally appear
on a film. We share screenplay credit on *Brady*
sequel. Everyone loves the movie but us. Funny
how these things turn around.

SEPTEMBER 1, 1996   JOURNAL ENTRY

Brady Sequel got some pretty good reviews,
but business was merely okay. I guess no third
film now. Time to move on.

Years later, on another trip to the Revolver Bar in Weho, the new
owner, my friend Chris Miller, said someone on the patio wanted to
meet me. He dragged me outside, and who should be standing there
but Maureen McCormick. Marcia, Marcia, Marcia! With her daughter. In a gay bar. Couldn't have been sweeter.

But then the conversation turned to why she didn't appear in our movies. She said she was never offered a part. What?!! We desperately tried to get her to do a cameo. Multiple times. The boys (Barry Williams, Christopher Knight, and Mike Lookinland) all jumped on board and seemed to enjoy poking fun at their famous roles. Somewhere I read that Maureen loves to sing country music, so we wrote a scene where she would be singing in a C&W bar. She still passed. Maybe she never got the scene. Who knows? It didn't matter at that point. I was instantly infatuated with her.

And if I'm being totally candid, I have to admit a completely embarrassing story about another original Brady girl.

In sixth grade, I wrote a school report about what I was going to do when I grew up. I was planning to move to Hollywood and marry Eve Plumb, "Jan Brady." So, of course, I nearly died when we had a casting session for our Lifetime sitcom, *Rita Rocks*, and I looked down at the list of women coming in to read for an upcoming guest star role. It was Eve. Jim begged me not to tell her the story of my school paper. I didn't. We kind of brought up that we wrote the *Brady Bunch Movies*, and she literally had no reaction. I got this "I don't want to talk about anything Brady" vibe from her. We let her read, and then she was out the door. My future bride-to-be. Gone in a flash.

I never understood why certain actors shy away from what made them household names. Shouldn't they be thankful they got a role that is so memorable?

A few years later, she came to see my TV theme show song musical, *It's On!*, in a staged reading in NYC because her friend Mindy Sterling was in it. After the show, Eve wanted to hang out with us. I didn't know what to expect, but then she was so nice and normal. Maybe she was having a bad day when she read for us earlier. Or maybe she was finally chilling out. Another example where I learned that the older I get, the more empathy I have for others. You never know what someone is going through.

Writing both *Brady Bunch* films was probably my favorite job ever because we were able to tap into all of our favorite things—camp, witty humor, and jokes that pushed the boundaries (but didn't cross them). Some of the craziness we got to play with were Mike's long stories, Marcia and Greg's sexual tension, and especially Marcia and Jan's sibling rivalry.

And we got to write for so many amazing women in the films— Jean Smart, Alanna Ubach, Henriette Mantel, Barbara Eden, Anne B. Davis, and friggin' Florence Henderson. C'mon—dream job!

But I still marvel how a two week job turned into a lifetime of Brady. And how some of our lines have now become memes, like "Sure, Jan." Not to mention T-shirts, mugs, etc.

Our dream would be to bring back Christine Taylor, Jennifer Elise Cox, and the wonderful Olivia Hack ("Cindy" or "Thindy") in a streaming series called *The Brady Ladies*. The show would focus on the three famous, blonde siblings moving to a West Hollywood apartment today, but still stuck in the past. The three actresses said they're on board. Now we need to get RuPaul to return as their landlord, Ms. Cummings. RuPaul would probably want to be the star of the show, much like Lucy Ricardo would try to steal the spotlight. That could be funny.

8

THE NEXT LUCY

During the late 80s and early 90s, television exploded with half-hour sitcoms. Some networks scheduled four on one night. "Must See TV." As a writer, you're lucky to have any job, let alone land on two acclaimed, massive hits, *The Golden Girls* and *Roseanne*. That made us desirable to the studios that started gobbling up writers to be put on overall deals. It was kind of like the old movie studio days: You signed deals that made you exclusive to one company. And you were given an office on the lot, an assistant, and an expense account. All that was expected of you was to develop new TV projects.

We signed multiple year contracts with Lorimar in Culver City and then moved with them to Burbank. After that came a few years with 20th Century Fox in Century City. Eventually we had our last big deal at Sony in Culver City. By the time we got there, the studios had gotten wise and put their term writers on existing shows that they owned to burn off some of the money they were already paying them. That's how we wound up on *The Nanny*. We felt very intimidated in their writers' room. The only fun part was the weekly trek out to Fran Drescher's Malibu house, hanging out over the beautiful Pacific Ocean. Loved her. And also loved when she asked if we wanted to get stoned. Of course we did!

Looking back on our many years in development, it probably would've been better for our careers if we'd continued being staffed on shows. We would've made more contacts that would be useful today. But we really enjoyed being on our own and having the chance to develop ideas with talent that WE wanted to work with. Naturally, we gravitated to working with women. Probably ninety percent of them said to us at some point during our initial meetings, "I want to be The Next Lucy." Of course, there could only be one Lucy. (Don't tell that to Nicole Kidman. Or her makeup/special effects people.)

Jim and I were fortunate to cross paths with many amazing women. We always thought Joan Collins had a dark sense of humor that wasn't quite utilized to its fullest comic potential as the conniving Alexis Carrington on *Dynasty*. She did a guest spot on *Roseanne*, but we thought her better suited for a single-cam comedy, which is shot more like a film.

Since people are crazy about anything to do with the royals, we came up with a show called *The Royal Life*. It would have the tone of a dark comedy like the movie *Dirty Rotten Scoundrels*. This was also when leads of network series had to be likable, so we knew it would be an uphill battle to sell it. That's why we made the heart of the show about a family. It so happened that the father, a king of a small island, got caught stealing large sums of money from the government. His wife (Joan Collins) and kids (the son would be someone like Rupert Everett) were forced to flee in disgrace. They come to the United States, Beverly Hills to be exact, with only their title to live off of. Or scam off of.

The first step was to pitch the idea to Lorimar's Comedy Development Team. Fortunately, they loved it and called Joan's agent. Joan was leaving the next day for her other home in London but would grant us an hour of her time to pitch to her. It was an unusually dark and rainy day as we drove up to her place in the hills of Bel Air. I was a little nervous because she had such an intimidating presence on screen.

APRIL 9, 1990   JOURNAL ENTRY

Last Wednesday, we had one of the best meetings. It was with Joan Collins. Pitched *The
Royal Life* and she loved it. Couldn't have
been lovelier. Laughed at all the right places. Now Lorimar is making the deal with her
and the networks. They think we'll just get a
pilot. I want six episodes. Please!

Jim and I both had trips planned to Europe, so I suggested we hop over to England to work with Joan on our pitch for the network. Jim and Joan were game.

When we rang the bell on her flat in a tony section of London, nobody answered. We wondered if we had the right address. We rang again. Suddenly someone picked up the intercom then buzzed us in. We sat in her parlor, waiting.

Eventually Joan enters in an oversized orange sweater, orange leg-gings, and I swear, her wig on sideways. We were convinced we had woken her from a nap. We wanted to learn more about her, so the character she'd be playing would fit her like a glove. Over tea, I started peppering her with questions about her past, hoping to engage her in conversation. She was having none of it. Alexis Carrington was now in the room.

Joan, snapping at me: "What are you, the bloody press hounding me for dirt?"

I wasn't going to let her get away with that. I decided to play *The Golden Girls* card.

Me: "We often pulled from the four ladies' real lives in order for the characters to have more verisimilitude. We thought you'd want that for your character."

She couldn't really argue with that.

The project ultimately fell apart. We never even got to take it to the networks. Joan wouldn't accept what Lorimar was willing to pay her for a holding deal. She wanted "hour" money and since this was a half hour, it wasn't even near what she was used to. I think this was shortsighted on her part. With this role (and show), she could've reinvented herself as a comedienne. I think it's still a funny idea.

Years later, my friend Peter Golden invited me to see Joan's one-woman show at Feinstein's at the Carlyle in New York City. After, we went backstage to say hello. Actually, there was no backstage. It was literally the kitchen. In between the pots and pans, she greeted me warmly, kissing me on both cheeks. She acted like she remembered me and was her delightful self again.

Instead of dealing with an established "star," I started searching for new talent on TV talk shows like *The Tonight Show*. There I became aware of country singer K. T. Oslin, an amazing singer/songwriter who signed a record deal at the age of forty-five. On her hit debut album, "80's Ladies," K. T. sang original songs she wrote from the POV of a mature woman. This was almost unheard of in country music. Or really any genre of music. But what really captivated me was her sense of humor. Self-deprecating, but still sensitive. I had to find out more about her.

At the office the next day, we did some investigating and learned that before moving to Nashville, K. T. had lived in Manhattan and pursued a career as a theater actress. She was even in the chorus of a few Broadway musicals, like *Promises, Promises*. She survived in the city by doing commercials for products such as toilet bowel cleaners. We showed her tape to the development people at Lorimar, and they agreed she had something special. After speaking with her agents, she decided to meet us and discuss developing a show for her.

They flew us to Nashville to convince K. T. (and her management) that instead of just touring, doing a sitcom would be a good idea. Once in Tennessee, we headed over to K. T.'s house. We found her in tears. Her dog was sick and near death. Not an ideal way to start a meeting. K. T., who had never married and had no kids, was extremely close to her pets. Being an animal person, Jim jumped in and quickly connected with her. Soon we were all drinking and getting a little more relaxed. We could make K. T. laugh, and she took a real shine to us. I'm not sure when we realized that we all enjoyed a little puff of pot, but that brought us even closer.

Back in LA, Jim and I came up with a show based on K. T.'s life called *Shirley Divan*. Shirley was described in our pilot script as "A vibrant woman decked out in colorful vintage clothing topped off with a flowing Lana Turner scarf." She was a middle-aged, not so successful, New York based actress (much like K. T.) whose biggest claim to fame was commercials. She returns to her hometown to take care of her sister's two kids after her sister is put in jail. K. T. flew out to LA to pitch to networks with us. She was great in a room, really letting her big personality shine.

DECEMBER 19, 1990   JOURNAL ENTRY

What a day! We got a pilot commitment for K. T. Oslin at NBC. After two years of development, I'm really happy. I love K. T.! A very complex, but wonderful person.

Unfortunately, NBC passed on the script. We didn't even get to film a pilot. I felt terrible. More for K. T. Like we let her down.

K. T. and I kept in touch for many years and talked on the phone a bunch. But then we lost touch.

Over her career, she had four no. 1 hits and placed many singles on the Billboard country charts, not to mention winning three Grammy Awards and being inducted into the Nashville Songwriters Hall of Fame. She did appear in the movie *A Thing Called Love* starring River Phoenix and Sandra Bullock. I would occasionally hear about health issues she was having, including being diagnosed with Parkinson's disease in 2015. That led to her moving into an assisted living facility. She died December 21, 2020, a week after being diagnosed with

COVID-19. She was 78 years old. She's buried in Nashville, across from Tammy Wynette. I miss her hearty, throaty laugh.

When you're on an overall deal with a studio, you're forced to meet with a lot of actors who already have network development deals. The first step would be an exploratory meet and greet. Usually in offices on the lot. That's where we sat with Shannon Doherty (and for some reason, her father), Marcia Cross, hot off *Melrose Place*, and Mary Hart of *Entertainment Tonight* fame. Not a comedienne in the bunch. We did like Lauren Holly and wrote a spec pilot based on an idea of hers. No one wanted to buy it. We learned a valuable lesson—find something organic that turns you on. You can't just chase a deal. But since we were under contract, we had to at least entertain the idea of working with all these women.

Sometimes we'd meet them at a restaurant of their choosing. Like Teri Hatcher at Art's Deli in Studio City. Although known for dramas, like *Lois & Clark*, she'd recently done a series of humorous commercials for Radio Shack with sports figure Howie Long, so the networks thought—THE NEXT LUCY.

She had one big concern. "It's really important to me to have a nice wardrobe on the show." Not exactly where we go first when developing a character.

One of my favorite meetings was with Pia Zadora at the famed Beverly Hills Hotel's Polo Lounge. This was so back in the day that no one had a portable cell phone yet. But Pia did. After all, she was married to gazillionaire Meshulam Riklis. This phone was bigger than a brick and just as heavy.

She placed it in the middle of the table because, she said, "I'm expecting a VERY important call that I cannot miss."

No call came in during our meal. I kind of felt bad for her. I should've pretended to go the bathroom and call her from a pay phone.

We did see Pia again. She invited us to the premiere party for her friend John Waters' latest film, *Cry Baby*. It was held at her huge house, known as the Pickford Estate after silent film star, Mary Pickford. It was super cool to see all the stars of the film at the party—Ricki Lake, Traci Lords, and even a young Johnny Depp.

I really enjoyed getting to know Michelle Phillips from the 60s singing group the Mamas and the Papas. I can still see the picture of the quartet squeezed into a bathtub on the cover of their debut album. Growing up, my mom constantly played it for us on our new stereo unit with separate, modern, modular standing speakers. She took great delight in knowing that I got friendly with Michelle and had numerous story meetings with her in restaurants across the San Fernando Valley. We had a cool hour show idea for her called *The Men in my Life*, kind of a reverse *Charlie's Angels*. She would play the "Charlie" character, a disgraced ex-spy who couldn't leave her house, so she got her pool boy, trainer, and gardener (all hot young men) to help her solve crimes. She pitched it to Aaron Spelling, and he liked it. But nothing ever materialized. Typical. But how's that for a full-circle moment?

It's always more fun to see a star in their own surroundings. To learn their decorating choices or what famous people were in framed photos on their mantels. Or which awards were displayed on their grand pianos.

One of those was Dyan Cannon. I was familiar with her work in such classic movies as *Bob & Carol & Ted & Alice* and *Heaven Can Wait*. And for having been married to Cary Grant. Dyan had just come off back-to-back comedic turns on *Ally McBeal* and an NBC sitcom, *Three Sisters*. NBC wanted to keep working with her, so off we went to her Brentwood house to pitch her show ideas, like two Willy Lomans from *Death of a Salesman*.

Surprisingly, we got to see the inside of Dyan's refrigerator. She sent us into the kitchen to grab Tupperware containers of cut vegetables—celery and jicama sticks. Before that I was a jicama virgin. She also had a tall bongo drum in the living room, which she straddled and proceeded to play during the pitch session. We got a Zen vibe from her.

Dyan: "I just love all your ideas. You boys are really clever. But . . ."

Her but was that she'd suggest another actress for each concept.

We wondered if she understood why we were there. We wanted HER to be the lead. Maybe she was in director mode since she had just helmed an indie movie and wasn't really thinking of herself. Or maybe she just wanted to collect the holding deal money from the network and had no real interest in making a pilot. We left having made a friend but with no commitment.

We also got to see the North Hollywood house of Ann Jillian (*It's a Living*) that she shared with her police sergeant husband; Suzanne Pleshette's glamorous high-rise West Hollywood apartment; Kathy Najimy's Hollywood Hills home where we sat in her backyard sipping tea; and Ellen DeGeneres's hip house in the Bird Streets above Sunset Boulevard when she was with Anne Heche. It was so odd sitting in their breakfast nook, watching the two lovebirds buzz around the kitchen, making us coffee.

Ellen later invited us to her office, along with a dozen other comedy writers. She wanted to pick our brains about creating a variety show for CBS, even though she couldn't sing or do characters. That show never materialized. Contrary to popular opinion, she was always nice to us, and I'd run into her a lot before she started her enormously successful talk show.

Jim and I were early fans of Whoopi Goldberg and always thought she'd be a natural for a sitcom. She responded to our material, so we were invited to her house just north of Sunset Boulevard in Beverly Hills. We pitched our little hearts out. She liked one about a school nurse who got into everybody's business, based on the Surgeon General at the time, Joycelyn Elders. Unfortunately, nothing came of that specific project, but a few years later we did go out with a pitch with her to produce. It was an hour musical show about an interracial love story taking place at the beach in the 60s between a young, Black teen girl surfer and a naïve White boy from the Midwest. We called it *Long Beach Blanket Bingo*. This was before *Glee*, and NOBODY wanted to do a TV show with music. Or one that dealt with racism. Even with Whoopi in a small part. We couldn't believe it. Once again, we were pitching shows that were way ahead of the time.

The high point was when we got a call from our agents to see if we'd meet with Diana Ross. Supposedly she was ready to "do TV" and was sitting down with writers." Were we interested?

"Are you insane?!" we said. "We're two gay men of a certain age. OF COURSE we'll meet her!"

I knew at the end of the day she would NEVER do a half-hour show, but I desperately wanted to see her up close. She was renting a house in The Hills, so off we went.

Suddenly, there we were knocking on Miss Ross's front door. It opened to reveal Diana looking casual, but fabulous. She asked us to sit in the living room with impressive views of the city below. Since this was a last-minute meeting, we didn't really have ideas prepared to pitch her. We all understood that this was more of an exploratory meeting to get to know one another. I was excited to tell her that I was born and raised in Detroit, hoping this would bond us, and I'd be her new best friend. She nodded politely. I kept going.

Me: "How did you feel when you saw your hometown on fire during the riots? I remember that day because I was in the car with my father and brother leaving a Detroit Tigers game, and I noticed huge clouds of black smoke in the rearview mirror. As soon as we got home, we turned on the TV and saw the riots were taking over parts of downtown."

Diana looked at me quizzically and said, "What riots?"

I was dumbfounded. Did she really not know about the Detroit Riot of 1967?!

Jim took over the meeting. The next thing I knew, we were back in our car, heading down the hill. She never did a pilot. Or even developed a script for one.

I did sit next to her daughter, Tracee Ellis Ross, on an airplane once. This was before *Girlfriends* or *black-ish*. We totally hit it off. I'm not at all surprised at her success. She's charming and funny and so down to earth. I would DIE to work with her one day.

The low point in our revolving door of meetings with female "stars" was when we had to sit down with Alisan Porter from the hit movie, *Curly Sue*. She was barely ten years old, so naturally she was accompanied by her mother. I'm sure she's a sweet person, but she was a LITTLE GIRL. Who made ONE MOVIE! All I kept thinking was—*What the hell happened to our career?!*

MAY 30, 1995   JOURNAL ENTRY

This past week was so crazy with TV offers. Much to the horror of our TV agents, we turned them all down. Everything—*Caroline in the City*, *Partners*, *The Crew*, etc. It was a tough decision, but unless it was going to be our own show, we wanted to take a stab at features.

At least that's what we planned on doing, but then Fox offered us an overall TV deal. We liked the security of a steady paycheck, and I loved having an office with an assistant. We packed our bags and moved to the 20th Century Studios lot in Century City. They housed us in a cool, corner office suite surrounded by writers on a new animated series, *The Simpsons*.

We started taking more meetings with actors who had development deals with networks, like Olivia d'Abo (*The Wonder Years*), who came to our office about eight-and-a-half months pregnant. NBC had signed her after a successful arc on *The Single Guy*, a Jonathan Silverman sitcom. I was so worried she was going to give birth right there in our office.

Pitching was becoming annoying to us, so we started writing pilot scripts on spec. One was *Elizabeth, New Jersey*, a female ensemble comedy about three young and struggling "Jersey girls." Elizabeth had dreams of breaking out of her blue collar life to become a lawyer, like Ally McBeal. Fox was interested in that script. We had a lot of fans there, especially the head of their comedy development department,

Theresa Edy. She had the best laugh in the business and such a kind heart. We befriended her when we were baby writers and she was starting out at CBS. I don't know what got into us, but when she asked us out for a business lunch, we said we'd take HER out. We told her we'd pick her up in front of her office at Television City. All she had to do was wear sensible shoes. We drove around the corner to Pan Pacific Park and had a whole picnic meal, with basket, checkered tablecloth, and even a bottle of wine. It made for an extremely memorable meal, and a strong bond was formed.

```
DECEMBER 18, 1995          JOURNAL ENTRY

Looks like FOX is going to give us a "put
pilot," meaning the network would guarantee
our pilot gets made or they'd have to pay a
substantial monetary penalty. All we'll have
to do is write a pilot for the singing group,
TLC. We'll probably be going to Atlanta to
meet with them in January. That will be a fun
trip.
```

In the end, we never went to Atlanta or wrote for TLC. The girls backed out of a deal. Then the studio called. "We just signed a deal with a young actor who's made a string of really popular, highly successful comedy movies, and we want you guys to meet him."

We were excited until they said his name—Pauly Shore. We didn't exactly share the same comic sensibilities.

Since they were paying us a lot of money, we agreed to at least sit down with him. He was actually a really sweet guy, so we agreed to move forward, but only if we could write it on spec. We didn't want to go to the networks and pitch with him. We wrote what we wanted and thought of it more as a movie feel than TV. It was about a pampered Beverly Hills young man whose fortune is threatened when his rich, widowed father meets a gold-digging, hot blonde with a young kid.

Think *War of the Roses* tone. Two networks wanted to make it, but since we were at 20th, they went with FOX. They felt that they had finally found the perfect companion piece to their long-running hit, *Married . . .with Children.*

Once the network greenlit our pilot, casting began. It was REALLY difficult, especially the role of Pauly's new "mom." We needed a smart actor to play someone dumb. Like Betty White so beautifully did as Rose Nylund. But this actor had to be a gorgeous, young, knockout. We found her in Charlotte Ross (*NYPD Blue*).

The reviews for "Pauly" were HORRIBLE. And although the initial ratings were good, after five episodes, FOX pulled the show. But we got so much out of the experience. Most importantly, we finally became "showrunners." We made great friends and new business associates. Now it was time to get on with the rest of our lives.

Unfortunately, Hollywood wouldn't let us. At least the television part of the business. The press was so brutal about Pauly Shore that they couldn't even see the show. They hated everything he stood for and carved him up and fed him to the lions. And the industry held us responsible. Nobody would even look at our scripts or our producing skills. When staffing for next season started, for the first time in our careers, we didn't get ANY offers. It was a splash in the face with cold water. And somewhat humiliating. We got to see who our true friends in the business were. After some wound licking, we decided to switch gears and refocus on our feature film career.

9

FEMALES ON FILM

The success of *The Brady Bunch Movie* opened many doors for us in feature films. Even more than after the bidding war for our spec feature, *The Ruthie Ruddick Story*. Now we had a produced film under our belt and a money maker at that.

We took a lot of meetings, many with women who had production companies with overall deals at studios. Let me correct that. We had meetings with many actresses' *development executives*. In the film world, it would be rare to actually sit in a room with a real movie star, so they'd have us first sit with their "Person." The closest we'd get to the actresses would be movie posters of them on their office walls staring down at us. Some of the offices we went to belonged to Drew Barrymore, Jennifer Garner, Jennifer Love Hewitt, Cher, etc.

On rare occasions, we'd get to meet with the actual actress. One was Jane Fonda. She pitched to US, not the other way around. She wanted to do a *9 to 5* kind of story, but instead of secretaries, she wanted to explore sexism with female flight attendants. I think that's what the movie was about. To be honest, I was so fixated on her piercing blue eyes and the fact that I was sitting on a couch talking with the legendary Jane Fonda, I'm not sure I heard a word she said.

Another movie star we got to meet in the flesh was Goldie Hawn. I was really excited since I was a huge fan of *Laugh-In*. And all of her movies. This was 1999, and she hadn't been in a film since the monster hit, *The First Wives Club* in 1996. Nobody really knew why. Was she simply picky? We heard she cowrote a female-buddy-spiritual-road comedy, but it never got off the ground. We had met her development exec, Teri Schwartz. They had a blind feature script deal with New Line since the studio was desperate for her to star in Warren Beatty's *Town & Country* movie. We hit it off with Teri, so the next step was getting Goldie to like us. Up to her house we went. It was in Beverly Hills, right across the street from Whoopi. Can you imagine the two of them meeting out by their garbage cans? What am I saying? I'm sure they have staff deal with those.

Once inside her home, we were taken to the kitchen, where there was a buzz of activity. Kurt Russell was in there. So was Oliver Hudson. A few other kids, not sure whose they were. We retreated upstairs to Goldie's meditation room. I was in heaven. She came in and sat cross-legged (natch) in a yoga position on the floor as we pitched our little hearts out. One idea was called *The Best Bitch*, about the cutthroat world of dog show competitions. (This was before *Best in Show*.) We'd read that Goldie loves dogs. She loved our pitch. New Line didn't. Back to the drawing board.

During our times together, she would often talk about her "Grammy" and mother and how much family meant to her. Especially her daughter Kate Hudson, who was about to make her acting debut in *Almost Famous*. Since we love female ensemble movies, especially those made by Nancy Meyers, we came up with a film about a divorced mom with three daughters, who (in our minds) would be played by Cameron Diaz, Drew Barrymore, and Kate Hudson. Can't you see it? They each were having personal relationship problems, and Goldie's character was experiencing love after giving up the thought of ever meeting a man again.

This was actually based on hearing my mom talk about dating after her painful divorce from my father. She said, "That part of my life is over." I always thought that was so sad. To give up on love.

Goldie liked the idea a lot and talked to Kate about it, who also liked it. As did New Line. We were in business. To make the characters feel rich and real, we asked if we could sit down with Goldie and Kate to hear real stories from them, like we did with Joan Collins.

I remember the four of us in Goldie's den on a cloudy LA afternoon. In chairs this time. We all drank herbal tea. For some reason, Jim sat behind me. It felt like I was a gay Oprah talking with a mother and daughter, who amazingly laughed and cried alike. Yes, I made them cry. It got that personal. And deep. We planned to put all that in our script, which we were calling *The Great Lakes*. The last name of the family was "Lake," and they had a beautiful summer home on Lake Michigan.

Goldie seemed thrilled with the outline, but then draft after draft, she'd pick at the littlest things. Pulling threads. There always seemed to be something wrong. There was no pleasing her. We felt a bit demoralized but then realized that's why she hadn't made many movies recently. She probably kept finding fault with scripts she was attached to.

After breaking the curse of adapting TV shows into films with *The Brady Bunch Movie*, we got offered every old series to take a swing at bringing to the big screen. Before that film, pretty much all of them failed at the box office (*The Beverly Hillbillies; Car 54, Where are You?; Get Smart*). We got offered *The Love Boat, My Favorite Martian, Gilligan's Island*, and others.

One gig we did go after hard was *Bewitched* at Sony. As a kid, I LOVED that show. It appealed to my campy, gay side I didn't even know I had at that age. I could also do a mean Paul Lynde impression. In fact, when they picked *Bye Bye Birdie* for the high school musical my senior year, I did my audition for Kim's dad, Mr. McAfee, completely in Paul Lynde's voice and mannerism. I got a lot of laughs. I did not get the part.

Our take on *Bewitched* was to write it as a modern-day love story but treat the witchcraft like an interracial love story. As an allegory. We also wanted to switch out "Darren," the husband character, halfway through the movie, like they did on the TV series. From Dick York to Dick Sargent. But without mentioning it in the story or acknowledging it in any way. We suggested starting with Dermot Mulroney, then switching to Dylan McDermott in the second half. We had lots of clever ideas like that. We didn't get the job. Nora & Delia Ephron did. Much bigger names. In my humble opinion, I don't think they had the right campy/gay sensibility of the TV show or that this movie needed. Might be time for a remake!

We did work with Betty Thomas again. Multiple times. Mostly to help fix scripts that she was attached to direct. We were flattered that she thought of us in that light. And it was always fun to come into a project as the "doctors." Usually at that point, they'd tried many stabs at the script and needed fresh eyes. She had us do a rewrite on *Signed, Sealed, Delivered*, a female action movie taking place at a postal office, and to star Ellen DeGeneres.

Our favorite job with her was a rewrite on a *Valley of the Dolls* remake. We titled it *Valley of the Dolls: The Relapse*. Betty had a brilliant take. The movie was about the making of a contemporary shot-by-shot remake of *Valley of the Dolls*, and slowly the actors cast in the "film" would start to become their characters from the original movie. Very meta. And also, very complicated to get the tone right. But if anybody could, the three of us could.

At this point, Betty and Jenno Topping (Alan Ladd's development exec) had created a company called Tall Trees, and they rented an entire house on Sunset Boulevard for their offices. We'd go there pretty much every day and work upstairs in one of the "bedrooms." They'd order in lunch (sometimes even dinner), and we'd talk through story points, then spend the rest of the day locked away writing.

While we toiled away, Betty started meeting actresses for the various lead roles. Like Beyonce as "Jennifer North," the Sharon Tate part. She had recently done *Austin Powers: Goldmember*, so we assumed she could do comedy. Britney Spears also came in for that role. You read right. And Katie Holmes as "Anne Welles," the Barbara Parkins's role.

How could I concentrate knowing those gay icons were across the hall, reading OUR lines? I begged to be in the room, but Betty thought that would be too intimidating for most of the actors. I did get to watch some of their taped auditions. Like Brittany Murphy as "Neely O'Hara," the Patty Duke role. Another one of my ideas. She was BRILLIANT. We wrote many drafts for Jennifer Lopez to play "Helen Lawson," the Susan Hayward part.

We did a table read at Betty's house in the hills. Kelly Preston was "Helen Lawson" and was surprisingly funny. And such a sweet person. Denise Richards was "Sharon Tate," and Taryn Manning read the Patty Duke role. I wish the world could've seen any of those wonderful actors in this movie.

Ultimately, 20th Century Fox didn't want to pay what it took to get a cast of that magnitude. They didn't think there would be an audience for this title. Are they nuts?! Most studios (and networks, for that matter) are in it for a surefire money maker. They rarely take chances. That's why it's so extraordinary that the *Brady* movies even got made. But I'm convinced it was because they were willing to commit to such a relatively small budget ($15m) for a major studio film.

The *Valley* gig did lead to another job at Fox, a rewrite of another TV show adaptation, *The Ghost and Mrs. Muir*. I loved the Hope Lange series growing up. We had a really cool take to modernize it. Think Sarah Jessica Parker as a Carrie Bradshaw-type who's afraid to write her second novel after having a monster runaway hit with her first. Her publishers send her off to a house on the East Coast where she falls in love with a ghost, a handsome, young JFK-type. Someone like Hugh Grant. Again, many drafts. Never got made. Maybe one day?

Another close call came in 2004 when we landed a rewriting gig for the film adaptation of the chick-lit book, *Fashionista*. The property was owned by Paramount and was being produced by Christine Peters. She had come off a massive success with the rom-com, *How to Lose Guy in 10 Days*, starring Kate Hudson and Matthew McConaughey.

Christine was also known as the ex-wife of Jon Peters, Barbra Streisand's famous hairdresser boyfriend. Then she supposedly dated Sumner Redstone. I guess she liked older, powerful (and rich) men. I should probably take a lesson or two from her.

Christine and her young development executive, Ollie Obst, really liked our take. And I've got to hand it to Christine, she came up with the idea of trying to attach Lindsay Lohan to star and produce. Lindsay was really big at that point with two hit movies—*The Parent Trap* and *Freaky Friday*. Jim and I were longtime fans of hers. Right after *Parent Trap*, we tried to get Lorimar to sign a TV deal with her as a little girl. But they didn't see what we saw.

Christine figured if Lindsay was attached, the studio would instantly greenlight the film. That's how the business works. Lindsay was supposedly interested in the project. Especially because it was centered in the fashion world, a passion of hers. But first Christine wanted to set up a meeting for the three of us. In true Christine fashion, it couldn't just be a normal office visit. Oh, no. Christine planned a big party at her home in the Hills, where Jim and I would "casually" hang out with Lindsay. She'd fall in love with us, then boom, a "Hollywood marriage" would be made.

Christine hadn't figured one part of the equation into the mix. Lindsay was now of drinking age. She was also now rich and successful and excited to take advantage of the wild LA night life. She never showed up at her own party. Her mother, Dina Lohan, continually called her cell. There was some screaming involved. And lots of hanging up. So, Christine sent us off to charm "the mom." And we did.

Later, we heard the whole project exploded after the party. Rumor has it that Christine might have charmed Lindsay's dad, Michael, a little too much. Or that's what Dina thought. Seems the Lohan family courts controversy. Which is a shame because I feel Lindsay has an inherent gift that's being wasted.

We didn't totally forgo TV and were able to sell a pilot here and there. One of them was a female ensemble comedy called *Steps*, about three stepmoms, that we developed with Jonathan Prince. Lifetime bought it, but we had sold a couple of other pilots while at Sony, so we gave that one to Jenji Kohan to write, and we supervised her. It was one of her first pilot scripts. She went on to create *Weeds* and *Orange is the New Black*. We started casting it, but then a writers' strike sadly put an end to that.

The other project we supervised was *4WD*, an animated pilot, also for Lifetime, and created by Sue Rose and Nahnatchka Khan (*Pepper Ann*). It stood for "four women driving" and was a female ensemble comedy about four coworkers who carpool to the office every day. Natch went on to create such shows as *Fresh off the Boat* and *Young Rock*. The network passed because their research found that "women don't respond to animation." I kid you not.

We were growing frustrated with television and sitcom pilot writing. Was the world telling us to throw in the towel? I wasn't ready yet. Maybe we needed to reinvent ourselves again. But how? And then the answer came from a small, curly-haired redhead.

10

THE SUN WILL COME OUT TOMORROW

While on our overall TV deal at Sony, they housed us in an office building on the Culver City lot. Down the hall from us were the prolific producing team of Craig Zadan and Neil Meron. We had met them socially, since, ya know, all gay people know each other. They had produced some highly acclaimed dramatic TV films, but their true love was theater. They started bringing old musicals to television, starting with Bette Midler in *Gypsy*, followed a few years later with Rodgers & Hammerstein's *Cinderella* for ABC with Whoopi Goldberg, Whitney Houston, and Brandy in the title role. That version was a big ratings hit, so Neil and Craig set their sights on a TV adaptation of *Annie*.

I loved the original Broadway production with Andrea McArdle when I saw it back in the day. But Jim and I didn't understand why it needed to be remade so close to the 1982 feature film version. That didn't stop Zadan and Meron from literally chasing us down in the parking lot one day. They told us they were looking for a quick punch up/rewrite because they had just cast Kathy Bates as "Miss Hannigan." Kathy had recently won an Oscar for Best Actress for *Misery*. They needed her lines to especially sparkle. Plus, Rob Marshall, who had choreographed *Cinderella*, was making his directorial debut. We wanted to work with that team, so we finally succumbed and said yes, even though we knew little about writing musicals. It would be a chance for us to reinvent ourselves one more time.

We got our marching orders from the network, producers, and director and went off to do our rewrite. Everyone loved our work. They thought our dialogue was sharp, funny, and right on the money. Except one person. Kathy Bates. She had it in her head that Carol Burnett was funny in the feature film version, and she wanted to play the role "darker." Out went all our finely crafted jokes.

We were still under contract, so they decided to have us help them fix Act Seven and focus on the characters of Rooster and Lily, since they had cast up-and-coming Broadway sensations Alan Cumming (*Cabaret*) and Kristin Chenoweth (*You're a Good Man, Charlie Brown*).

When we saw them in rehearsals, we discovered they were performers that seemed to have a light bulb inside. You could tell they would be big stars. On set, Kristin was being chased by every network to star in her own sitcom. The "suits" were constantly coming by the set to check her out. Jim and I talked at length with Kristin about how to navigate sitcom development. We secretly wanted the gig. She seemed open about that too. But alas, NBC had other plans. And that was the end of that. We were there to do a job, and we were proud of our work on that TV movie. It won a Peabody Award, and many people think it's the quintessential version of that musical.

The success of that job started opening doors for us in the musical world. Especially with Zadan/Meron and ABC. They had us jump into their next TV movie musical adaptation, *The Wiz*. Everyone agreed that the music from that show was brilliant, but the book (that's what they call the script for a musical) could use some major tweaking. They hired Rob Iscove, who had choreographed *Annie*, to be the director. And Paula Abdul to choreograph.

I started going to dancer auditions at the now defunct Debbie Reynolds Studios in the Valley. That's where I befriended Paula. It's no secret she's VERY emotional, and she needed a shoulder to cry on when she felt belittled by Rob. He had a tough demeanor. But strangely enough, he took a shining to me and Jim and rarely showed that side of his personality to us.

STAN ZIMMERMAN   139

The team of Zadan & Meron were able to attach an amazing star-studded cast:

Aunt Em—Audra McDonald

Scarecrow—Alan Cumming

Tin Man—John Leguizamo

Lion—Brian Stokes Mitchell

Glinda—Sherie Rene Scott (I got to meet her after a matinee of *Aida* on Broadway)

Evillene—Lillias White; and introducing

Dorothy—Anika Noni Rose (yes, in her first filmed role)

The network decided, for budgetary reasons, to shoot in Budapest. Rob was sent there to scout locations.

Then, all of a sudden, the plug was pulled on the project. Theater producers that held the stage rights didn't think it would be advantageous for a TV production to be made. They thought it would cut into their ticket sales. That was the thinking back then. Subsequently, it's been proven the exact opposite, with movies of shows like *Chicago* able to bring more audiences to Broadway and touring companies because so many more people are familiar with the title now. But what Jim and I were both dumbfounded about was that NO ONE from ABC or their crackerjack legal team knew about this clause in their rights' contract? How do you spend ALL that money on a project, get that close, and THEN discover this? We obviously were extremely disappointed.

We did get to work with Neil and Craig one more time. They asked us to create a *Grease* reunion TV movie, which we named *Grease: Still the Word*. They, along with Didi Conn (as a producer), wanted to focus on the kids of Rydell High from the movie, with a few parts of their parents played by the original film cast. This movie would be set in the 80s. We devised the plot so that "Sandy" (Olivia Newton-John) spent most of the movie hoping "Danny Zuko" would show up at a

Rydell High reunion. The climax would be John Travolta getting off an airplane, which we added since we knew he loves flying, taking a limo to the gymnasium, and having one last dance with Sandy. Travolta was a big movie star then, so we thought he might agree to do a TV movie if there were only a few scenes to shoot. We also had Stockard Channing's character, "Rizzo," return from Hollywood for the event. Rizzo was now an actress and up for the part of "Alexis Carrington" on *Dynasty*. Right before the reunion starts, she learns she lost the role to Joan Collins. In her hotel room, depressed and humiliated, she'd sing a torchy/sad song in the vein of "There Are Worst Things I Could Do." We had lots of other thought-provoking plot lines like that. But then—

MARCH 26, 2002   JOURNAL ENTRY

We found out that ABC's bailing on our *Grease* reunion TV movie. Didi Conn and Paramount don't like the direction of the script. Quinn Taylor (head of TV movies at ABC), Neil, and Craig do. I guess Quinn doesn't feel like it's worth all the aggravation.

By now, we were getting used to this career roller coaster ride. We'd trained ourselves to roll up our sleeves and move on after a big disappointment. But what to write next? A movie? TV pilot? As I learned from reading Shirley MacLaine's spiritual books, trust the universe, and soon we had our answer. The world had other plans for us, and another big opportunity arose. It was still writing a musical, but this one would be for the stage. Although theater doesn't pay as much as TV and film, Jim was still open to meeting on it. It was with Immortal Records, a music company that wanted to create a stage show about the relationship between Elvis and Priscilla Presley.

Now I have to admit, we weren't Elvis freaks. We knew some of his music and story, but we had to do a lot of research. We came back to the development execs (Matt Weaver and Janet Billig Rich) with our take for the piece. They loved it, so the next step would be to pitch it to Priscilla herself. I was looking forward to it because I liked her from the *Naked Gun* movies. And, well, she's kind of an icon. By this time, Jim and I had become expert pitchers, and she must have responded to our take on the show and our easygoing, fun manner. We landed the job! Even over Pulitzer Prize winning playwright, Suzan-Lori Parks. That surprised us. We were calling it *Burning Love* and making it about Elvis and Priscilla's unique love story from *her* point of view.

Priscilla was lovely and suggested it might help if we saw Graceland in person. We had a funny tour guide character as the "Narrator" of the piece. We thought we could stunt cast it with someone like Rosie O'Donnell. We chose that device since we learned that Graceland was in such disrepair that it was going to be sold, until Priscilla took it over and turned it into one of the most successful tourist destinations in the world.

Priscilla agreed to meet us in Memphis and be our tour guide. Jim and I went a few days early to do our own digging. We discovered this super-cute restaurant that used to be an old beauty parlor, naturally called The Beauty Shop Restaurant. Coincidentally, this was the actual salon where Priscilla would get her famous, teased, beehive hairdos done. We called Priscilla and told her to meet us at their address the next day for lunch but didn't tell her about her history with the place. And we didn't let the restaurant owners know who was about to arrive.

When Priscilla walked in, the staff literally stopped in their tracks. They tried to play it cool, but soon they were all coming over to our table to pay their respects. She handled it with such grace and was so fun on that trip. She even made self-deprecating comments about taking us to a Scientology building. Yes, she was a Scientologist at the time. We didn't go. We did end up at a farm outside of Memphis that was Elvis and Priscilla's little getaway. On the corner of the large property now sat a tiny florist shop. We told our driver to pull over.

We went in first, and Priscilla followed shortly thereafter, with sunglasses and a scarf on. We encouraged the owner to tell us about his store. He launched into stories about Elvis and Priscilla, then suddenly took a look at Priscilla and saw that it was actually her, in the flesh, standing there. He nearly fainted.

The next day, Jim and I planned to take the regular tour of Graceland, then at night Priscilla would return with us and we'd get a once in a lifetime tour by her, including going upstairs and other places on the property that were off limits to regular tourists. But later that day, Priscilla called and said she wasn't emotionally up for going back at night. She didn't want to be in the house in the dark, with all those memories and smells. I was disappointed but understood how tough that would've been for her.

We got to take another trip with Priscilla. This one to New York to see a few Broadway shows because she wasn't familiar with the musical form and wanted to learn everything. I was impressed. She said she was often viewed by others as not very savvy as a businesswoman and had to constantly prove to people how smart she was.

We accompanied Priscilla to see a few shows, including the last preview of *Wicked*. When we were leaving the theater, she asked me and Jim to flank her, one on each side. We weren't sure why but did as requested. As we walked from the theater to her waiting limo, out of nowhere, paparazzi jumped out from behind pillars to take pictures of her.

Once inside the safety of her car, she explained, "This kind of thing happens to me all the time. They do it to get a shocked look on my face and hopefully an embarrassing picture, which they then sell to the tabloids for a lot of money. The crazier my expression, the more money they make."

They've been hounding her like this since she met Elvis as a young teen. As we got to know each other better, she began to open up a little more. She revealed that Elvis told her not to trust ANYONE. That people might only talk to her to get to him. Especially the girls in her senior year of high school in Memphis. That's why she remains so guarded in her personal life to this day. But somehow, she still seemed to be a genuinely good person who really cared about others.

Back in LA, we worked on our next draft of the script. Once Priscilla got a chance to read it, she called us to her house in the Hollywood Hills for a notes meeting. Her assistant led us into a small study, then went to tell Priscilla we had arrived. Inexplicably, Jim and I simultaneously turned our heads to the hallway. Then we looked at each other.

"Did you just see that?" I whispered.

He nodded his head.

I asked him what he saw.

He whispered back, "A shadowy figure cross down the hall."

I said, "Like the presence of Elvis?"

He nodded again. We both got up and looked. There was no one in the hall. We were kind of spooked, and it must've shown on our faces because when Priscilla came downstairs, she asked, "Are you guys okay?"

I hesitantly said, "Um, by chance, did you live in this house when Elvis was still alive?"

She said she did, then added that he would occasionally come banging on the door late at night, drunk or high, wanting to see his daughter, Lisa Marie. Priscilla would have to calm him down and get his driver to take him back home.

So, yes, that day we saw the ghost of Elvis Presley, and I'm sticking by that story.

The last time I saw Priscilla was when she invited us to her sixtieth birthday party at a restaurant in West Hollywood. I couldn't believe I was sitting there with Lisa Marie, who knew who I was. Like most of our projects during that time period, nothing ever happened with it. Being compensated for our work was important to us, and to me being able to pay my mortgage and stay in my house, but we desperately wanted to see our vision come to fruition. I still think our concept could make for a captivating musical show, even though I'm not sure how people would view Elvis starting a relationship with an underage girl. But if they can make a hit musical out of Michael Jackson's story, I guess anything is possible.

We thought maybe it was time to go back on a TV show. But after so many years on studio deals, we didn't have many friends running shows. Until, once again, a woman came to our rescue.

11

WELCOME TO STARS HOLLOW

You can make a good living writing for television and film without having your scripts produced. But it grew frustrating, if not downright demoralizing. We knew we were lucky. Most writers in town don't get ANYTHING produced. But we wanted to catch a break after a string of "nos" and so many major disappointments. I wondered whether we should go back to being on staff for a sitcom, but Jim was at a different place in his life. He didn't like the long hours and was enjoying being able to travel whenever he wanted. He wasn't worried about money like I was because he had family income coming in. That's why he didn't even want to entertain the idea of going back on staff.

But then we got a call from our old *Roseanne* pal, Amy Sherman. She was now officially Amy Sherman-Palladino, or ASP, since marrying Dan Palladino. We went to their wedding and hung out quite a bit after *Roseanne*. We'd help her punch up pilots and even gave her new show ideas but stopped seeing her regularly when she got busy with *Gilmore Girls*.

We weren't sure why she was asking us to meet her and Dan for drinks at the famed Chateau Marmont. I loved that hotel and its old school vibe. It was built in 1929 and was having a resurgence of popularity with the young, hip Hollywood crowd. Over martinis, Amy told us about all the problems she was having with the WB executives. She was also having trouble finding writers who could execute her vision, which was very specific. She was cleaning house (again) and bringing on a whole new staff of writers.

Amy: "I want friends around."

She wondered if we'd ever consider leaving the lucrative world of development to come work on staff. I was sure Jim would say no. But he always really liked Amy and agreed to take the discussion to the next step, only for a year. And if we'd have a mutual option to continue if we were all happy. I was excited for myriad reasons. I missed going to an office. And being on a show. And honestly, the consistent money would be fantastic.

I told Amy if we took the job, "I'd make it my personal mission to keep you happy for that year. There's no reason you shouldn't be. You finally have a hit show that's well respected in the community."

This was a role I was accustomed to, much like how I had to cheer up my depressed mom during her difficult divorce.

MAY 27, 2004   JOURNAL ENTRY

Big news—we were officially offered a job on *Gilmore Girls*. After four years of Amy never mentioning it, now she wants us. We're in negotiations to join Season Five. I feel so conflicted about it. Not quite ready to give up my lovely life to work 10:30-7 five days a week until APRIL! Yikes.

Amy told us she was bringing on Bill Prady to run the room when she and Dan were on set. I knew Bill from Kennedy Elementary School. We were really good friends from fourth through sixth grade but lost touch as adults. He was coming off years on *Dharma & Greg*. I thought he'd be perfect for *Gilmore Girls* since he's super smart in a brainiac kind of way. Which makes sense since he would go on to co-create *The Big Bang Theory* a few years later with Chuck Lorre (a

Roseanne alum). We agreed to a consulting producer credit, so as not to ruin our quote for executive producer.

Per Amy's instructions, we were asked to watch EVERY episode that had aired. She wanted us to get caught up with all the storylines before we started work. I think I had only watched the pilot, so that meant four seasons' worth of shows to view. Two huge, long boxes arrived at my door from the studio. This was before DVDs, so there were literally eighty-seven videocassettes that I'd have to get up from the couch and insert into my VCR.

I locked myself in the house and sat down with pen and paper, ready to take notes. And lots of coffee. Which was fitting for that show. I wasn't sure how I could physically get through all those in one weekend. Without losing my mind.

I decided I'd start by rewatching the pilot, which I found to be beautifully constructed. The idea that Lorelai and Rory were forced to have a weekly Friday night dinner with Lorelai's parents that they were both estranged from was utterly brilliant. And to have such distinguished film/theater actors like Kelly Bishop (*A Chorus Line*) and Edward Hermann in the roles of "Emily and Richard Gilmore," I was impressed.

But the heart of the show was Lorelai and Rory. A mother and daughter who were more like friends. I have to admit I fell in love with Lauren Graham the minute she came on screen. She's obviously a true beauty, but her comic timing, wit, and intelligence were off the chart. And newcomer, Alexis Bledel, was so natural, she had a way of drawing you in. You couldn't take your eyes off either one of them. You also couldn't let your ears rest for one second since they talked so damn fast. Amy wanted the show to have the speed of those old 40's madcap comedy films. And she also used a sitcom technique of buttons to end scenes, which is rarely used in hour shows. All this added up to make *Gilmore Girls* such a unique show. What started as a chore for me to watch quickly became addictive.

Television series writing usually starts in June, so you can get a jump on scripts before a show premieres in the fall. Once episodes start airing, it's a game of catch up. And keeping your strength up because it's so exhausting. You're breaking stories, while also writing your own episodes, while also rewriting others, and casting and editing others.

Although Amy and Dan lived in this super-fabulous, two story, Mediterranean house in Hancock Park, they rented a big modern home on the beach in Santa Monica. We were required to drive out there all summer, Monday through Friday, to work on mapping out the first half of the season.

On Day One, Jim and I met in a parking lot near their house so we could walk in together. We hadn't been on staff in a long time and didn't know quite what to expect. We got there early in case there was traffic. We sat in Jim's car and went over the "what ifs" like I had done with my mother before nervously starting a new school year.

Suddenly, we saw this beautiful blonde girl in a short peasant dress with a big floppy hat and sandals. She was a vision out of a 60s foreign film. Twenty minutes later, we'd learn that it was Rebecca Kirshner (*Buffy, the Vampire Slayer*), another writer on the show. Besides her and Bill Prady, there was Jessica Queller (*One Tree Hill*), who spent a good portion of the time under a blanket on the couch. Of course, we gravitated toward the women writers. And also the writer's assistant, Lisa Randolph. Writer's assistant is such a tough job, and Lisa was a superwoman. And funny as hell. She became our bestie, and we'd always have lunch together and get into a little trouble on the lot. She'd been on *Gilmore* for a couple seasons and knew where all the bodies were buried. But Jim and I had to let the others on staff know that even though we were Amy's friends, they could say anything around us. We were not going to run and tell her. And we didn't.

For two and a half months, we'd go out to their beach house. They'd lock us in this room and close the shutters, so we couldn't even see the beautiful sand and water. All we could look at was this whiteboard. At first, we discussed arcs for the characters.

Amy wanted Season 5 to be about couples coming together and breaking apart and then finally, by the end, be back together again. I thought this was supercool. I also loved how she would plant a seed in an early episode, then that seed would eventually blossom into a full-fledged story in a future episode. That's not normal for series writing. Usually, stories are self-contained in each episode.

The room was tense. Amy and Dan didn't seem to really like any of Bill's suggestions. I'm not even sure they needed a writers' room since they had such a firm grasp on what they wanted. So, there we all had to sit. Hours on end. The only time we got a break was when we went to the bathroom. I would take as long as I could without raising suspicions of bladder problems. It's funny—it's the exact opposite of my time avoiding bathrooms in junior high. Now, I couldn't wait to get to one.

I really enjoyed when we moved to the Warner Brothers lot. Our office became the social hub where the staff would come to hang. We kept our office door open, and every morning Amy (and Dan), not always arriving together, would pass by it.

I'd smile big and wave and say, "Morning!"

No response. Nothing. Not even a wave. She'd just keep walking. At first, I was hurt by this but soon realized I shouldn't take it personally. This was simply her way.

My way is different. I think it's important when you're the showrunner, or a boss in any job (really, in life), to be nice and say hello. And especially "thank you" to EVERYONE. People will work harder for you if they feel appreciated and part of a team. And it just makes for a more pleasant atmosphere. Especially if you have to be together all day and sometimes long into the night.

Except for that morning weirdness, Amy was great with me and Jim. She is known for totally rewriting everyone's script. She'd cover her desk with candles and stay up all night, putting the script through her brain. A complicated, but genius, brain. The scripts always turned out better. And more layered. And smarter. And funnier.

For whatever reason, a lot of our words stayed in our scripts. But boy, was it hard to write them. Most hour shows are maybe sixty-some pages. Think a minute per page. *Gilmore Girls* scripts were seventy-five to ninety pages because the characters talked so damn fast. What helped me in the writing was how I could draw upon the relationships I saw between my grandmother, mother, and sister. They definitely shared similarities with Emily, Lorelai, and Rory.

Although we had our name on two pivotal scripts, "Pulp Friction" and "Norman Mailer, I'm Pregnant," when you write on staff, you have your hands in all of the scripts in a season. Eventually, you forget which lines you contributed to each.

Amy also did something unusual for an hour show: She'd have table reads of the next week's script on the Friday before they'd start shooting. When we arrived for our first table read, on one of the golf carts that are all over studio lots, I saw Lauren Graham standing in front of her truck smoking a cigarette, like Lorelai Gilmore would do. I marched right over to her. I had to. I wanted to gush but played it cool. I didn't want to come off as a weirdo.

She was shocked that I approached her so brazenly.

Lauren: "You better not let Amy see you. She doesn't like writers talking to the actors. You might get fired."

I wonder if Amy picked that up from Roseanne.

I shot back, "Let her fire me. We're only here for the year. I'd gladly take the paychecks and stay home."

Lauren loved my snappy attitude, and soon we became friends, on and off the set. I was also someone she could vent her occasional frustration to since I had a history with Amy. But we also had mutual respect and much admiration for Amy, so it never got petty or dramatic. Purely normal bitch-about-work talk.

Amy knew I wanted to be a director, and she had me read the stage directions at all the table readings. I was never sure which action lines to say since I didn't want to break up the flow of the fast-paced dialogue. My stomach would be in knots knowing I had to do this every week. And if Lauren kept talking, I had to follow her lead and shut up. I soon learned to roll with it.

For many of the readings, Kelly and Ed would be on the conference room speakerphone since they lived back East and weren't in every episode. A couple times, we had Milo Ventimiglia and Jared Padalecki at the readings. Both were so nice and SO cute. One time, I'm not sure why, but Alexis literally picked me up and carried me around the room in her arms. This was odd, since she was a thin young woman. And I had been warned how shy she was. But for me, it wasn't unusual because I'm often picked up physically at bars when I go out. Like a human beach ball. For some reason people feel the need to lift me in the air. I guess it's a compliment?

Speaking of cute, young men, we all knew we needed one to play Logan Huntzberger, Rory's new love interest at Yale. And he had to be a really good actor given that he'd have a major story arc throughout our entire season. The casting office was right outside the writers' room, so we'd often see actors waiting to audition for Jami Rudofsky and Mara Casey, the show's casting director team.

One morning, while heading into the room, I saw two young, adorable actors sitting across from each other on couches. My eyes went to the blond one.

Once in the writers' room, I asked Amy, "Who are those guys?"

Amy: "Our final two callbacks to play 'Logan.'"

I blurted out, "You have to hire the blonde one!"

That was Matt Czuchry.

Amy: "Why?"

Me: "I don't know. I just have this feeling. Plus, I think his coloring would look great opposite Alexis."

And he did. He also felt very "old money."

So, even though I don't approve of all his character's choices in later seasons and the reboot, I'll always be "Team Logan."

Years later, I ran into Matt in NYC in an elevator going up to a party for the TCA (Television Critics Association). I told him he owed his entire career to me and that I'm going to take full credit for all his success. We had a good laugh. I was only half kidding.

Another selling point Amy made to me when we initially met with her and Dan at the Chateau was that I'd get to be on set a lot. I was secretly hoping maybe one day I could direct an episode. Unfortunately, we rarely went down there. Once for the cake cutting for the 100th episode celebration. And once to say hello to Norman Mailer when he was filming our script. We felt we couldn't leave the writers' room. We had such a small staff, there would've been a big hole if I left the room. And Jim didn't want to be in there alone. Also, Bill Prady, who was supposed to be running the room, kind of threw in the towel and would sit by the window and sadly look out. I think he felt beaten down after months of Amy and Dan not being especially receptive to him. I felt bad.

JUNE 16, 2004   JOURNAL ENTRY

Work on *Gilmore* is getting better, but I still feel like I'm not getting to use all my creative juices. The job is very strange. We did have a great dinner with Amy last week. Just the three of us. Got way too stoned and ate at the Firefly. And laughed. Harder than I have in years.

Except for the table reads, we didn't really have much interaction with the actors on the show. Sometimes they'd swing by our offices. Melissa McCarthy would come sit with us on the picnic tables outside in the back of our office building. She wasn't a "star" then, merely a friend hanging out on a work break. I remember her being so funny and down to earth.

We also knew Emily Kuroda, "Mrs. Kim," from our days writing on *Gung Ho*. She's an exceptional actor, and I love that she always returns to the stage to share her talents with live audiences.

And Bill Prady was not the only one from my hometown of Southfield, Michigan, who was involved with the show. I knew Rose Abdoo, who played "Gypsy," from my high school. How crazy is that?

A common question I get asked about the show—"Is there any storyline we pitched that was NOT put in?"

I have to say that Jim and I wanted Michel, played by Yanic Truesdale, to have a boyfriend or some love interest in Stars Hollow. We were shocked when Amy said Michel wasn't gay. Had she ever watched the show? For some reason, she didn't want to go there with the character. I did notice in the Netflix reboot Michel had come out of the closet. Little victories.

One day at work in our office, a call came through. It was Scott Henderson, a big talent agent at William Morris. I thought he was calling to pitch an actor for *Gilmore Girls*.

Scott: "I'm calling about *you*. And your writing partner. I want to know if you guys would be interested in meeting to be the showrunners/hosts on a new Bravo reality show called *Situation: Comedy*. It's being produced by my client, Sean Hayes. It's a competition show to find the next great sitcom."

I remained calm on the outside, but inside I was dying. I LOVE reality TV. At that point, I think I had watched every single episode of MTV's *The Real World*. Not to mention being obsessed with *American Idol*.

Me: "Let me talk to Jim, but we'd love to set up a meeting to come in and talk about it."

I hung up and nearly exploded, I was so excited. Jim was skeptical, which caught me by surprise. He loved reality shows as much as I did. Somehow, I talked him into going in for the meeting.

One of the execs in the room was a young Andy Cohen. This was at the beginning of the first *Real Housewives of Orange County* season. I didn't realize this was like an actor's audition. Otherwise, I would've been petrified.

We were offered a job as "showrunners" on a
Bravo reality show. Jim doesn't want to do it.
I hate that he's taken the fun out of getting
this job. I'm not even sure why he doesn't
want to do it. Maybe it has something to do
with not wanting to be caught on camera not
doing a good job. Or how he will physically
look on camera. I don't know. But it has really shaken me.

I was so hurt that Jim didn't want to take this job. I felt it could
elevate us as a team in the eyes of the industry. After all our many years
in television, networks still didn't view us as capable of running a show.
We would always have to attach a big writer/producer to our pilots. I
felt that this would finally let us be the "elephant in the room." This led
to some pretty intense fights unlike any before. But he was firm. He
wouldn't do it.

For the first time, I could see our partnership ending. And we had
worked so hard for so many years and had come so far together. Would
it be the end of our friendship too? It was that bad. But something
inside me said not to let this opportunity go by. I wracked my brain
to figure out a solution. I even offered up myself, solo, for the gig. But
Bravo really liked the idea of "casting" a team. Mind you, this all went
on while we're working on *Gilmore Girls,* and I couldn't tell Amy or
anyone on staff about it.

Then I had a brainstorm. I knew this veteran TV comedy writer,
Maxine Lapiduss (*Roseanne, Ellen*), through Allee Willis. I was in my
car, driving on Mulholland Drive, hands free—relax, Oprah!—when I
called Maxine.

First thing out of my mouth was, "How would you like to star in
a TV show with me?" Well, she jumped at the opportunity. So, back to
Andy Cohen we went.

SEPTEMBER 29, 2004   JOURNAL ENTRY

It looks like Maxine Lapiduss and I will be doing the Bravo show. But I'm still disappointed
in Jim. Wish it didn't continue to hurt.

I knew I had to tell Amy I was doing the Bravo show, not ask her. There would be certain days that I would have to miss part of work. I was so worried that she'd think it was stupid, lowering myself to "do reality." I asked her if we could go to her office to talk privately.

Once there, I expressed my deep desire to do this.

Me: "Plus, Jim would be in the room covering for me. And it would be less than two months where I'd be doing double duty. I really want to do this."

She kind of shrugged, rolled her eyes, and said, "Sure. Why not?"

I wasn't expecting it to go that smoothly.

Then I had to tell the writers. I didn't want them to feel like I was leaving them in the lurch. Luckily, they all seemed intrigued.

Somehow, I managed to do a lot of writing in my journal during this crazy time.

OCTOBER 21, 2004   JOURNAL ENTRY

Have to be up at 6 a.m. My call time is 7:30
a.m. Love saying that! Tomorrow is the first
shoot for the Bravo show. I'm so excited! Not
that scared, surprisingly. I've been waiting
my whole life for this moment. Buckle up! This
is going to be a ride!

NOVEMBER 4, 2004   JOURNAL ENTRY

After working all day on *Gilmore*, I went to a
7 p.m. shoot for *Situation: Comedy*. They flew
in nine contestants from all over the United

States. They pitched their pilot ideas to us;
then we held five back to pitch to NBC executives tomorrow. I had a big role in the show.
I was the one to announce who would stay and
who would be sent packing. I had watched Ryan
Seacrest very carefully over the years, so I
had it down.

Later, everyone said I did a great job. I
felt really good. It was hard to come home
alone. And to fall asleep. I don't really have
anyone special to tell all this to. My mom,
maybe. I can't even explain all the emotions
that are going on right now. I feel so alive!
Not scared. Almost like I'm meant to do this.
All my training and experience has worked up
to this moment. But where will it lead? The
possibilities are endless. It's so exciting.
Sean Hayes wanted to know if I was single. He
couldn't believe that I was. He said he'd be
on the lookout for me.

NOVEMBER 22, 2004   JOURNAL ENTRY

What a week! 7:45 a.m. calls for the Bravo
thing, racing to *Gilmore* at Warners at 11,
working there all day, running back to Sunset
Gower Studios around 7 p.m. and working on
Situation: Comedy till after 11 p.m. Then I
go home, take a bath, climb into bed and do
notes on a script on both shows, then sleep
and start all over again. I'm not complaining
because I'm having the time of my life! A
surreal time with the cameras and wearing a
mic all the time. Luckily, Amy has been great
about the whole thing.

DECEMBER 19, 2004   JOURNAL ENTRY

Only three more crazy days. I don't know how
I've done it. I just kept going and don't
think too much about it. It shows how you can
do anything if you put your mind to it. And
it's been one of the most rewarding experiences I've ever had. And there's been a lot.

JANUARY 31, 2005   JOURNAL ENTRY

What a month! I need it to be over. I think I
was at my boiling point on Sunday. I thought I
was past working on weekends, but there I was
on the Warners lot. I can't really complain,
but I am ready to slow down a bit. So happy the
season is over soon. But then what? Talking
with Amy about coming back to Gilmore, but
only three days a week.

AUGUST 8, 2005   JOURNAL ENTRY

Amazing premiere party for *Situation: Comedy.*
Great energy in the room. Sat with Lauren Graham
most of the evening. Mom was there and smiling
proudly. The only downside has been the ratings. Dismal. Actually, beyond dismal. Bravo
moved our time slot twice. Then Sean washed
his hands of it. But I have to focus on all the
good that came of it. A newfound strength.

The ratings were so bad for *Situation: Comedy*, that they wanted to
scrap a big finale. I told them they had to announce the winner and
pitched to them a cheap last episode. Just have me, Maxine, and Sean
Hayes on a couple couches, and we'd interview the contestants and
show clips. Hmmm, I wonder where Andy Cohen got the idea for his
Real Housewives reunion shows . . .

We didn't go back to *Gilmore Girls*. Jim was ready to move on and start developing our own material again. I feel like our writing style forever changed after spending a year in Stars Hollow. We learned a lot from Amy, especially the idea of planting seeds in early episodes that could then be used as future stories. That made one's storytelling feel so much more organic.

As much as I loved the characters on *Gilmore Girls* and some of the people on the show, it wasn't a "fun" working atmosphere. We were both getting to a point in our lives, maybe it had to do with maturing, but we wanted to feel appreciated. I unexpectedly found a road to that when I was at dinner with the producers of *Situation: Comedy*, Sean Hayes and Todd Milliner. Also at the table was Todd's boyfriend, Michael Matthews. Michael was artistic director of Celebration Theatre, the longest running LGBTQ theater in America.

Michael asked if I ever thought about directing.

"Sure!" I said, practically spitting out my martini.

He wondered if I'd want to direct for their theater, and we all started throwing out possible play titles that would be right for my maiden endeavor. He suggested I direct live episodes of *The Golden Girls*. I told him Witt-Thomas-Harris would never allow that, but I was still interested.

Two days later, I emailed Michael a list of play ideas. At the top was *Gemini* by Albert Innaurato. It was one of the longest running plays on Broadway. I had seen it while a student at NYU. It was the first "gay play" I saw, and I remember feeling nervous that people in the audience would know I was gay. I had also figured out that this could be a thirtieth anniversary production of the play.

Michael was all in. Landing that gig changed the trajectory of my life. That's why I tell my acting students to always say—"Yes, and . . .," not just for improv sketches but for everyday use. If I'd let the opportunity pass with *Situation: Comedy* when Jim wouldn't do it, I probably wouldn't be so involved in theater today. Returning to the stage has meant EVERYTHING to me. It's literally given me life.

Although I told Michael I wanted to direct, I didn't reveal that I didn't know how. Off I went to Samuel French Book Store (sadly now closed). I found Harold Clurman's book, *On Directing*, and have used his words of wisdom for every play I direct. He said to read the script multiple times, through the eyes of each character, since each actor comes to the director with specific questions about their motivation. A useful tool that most writers don't even think about.

We jumped right into casting. I had to use my Rolodex of actor friends since the theater didn't have many people submit to audition. I started with one of the most brilliant and hysterical actors I know, Stephanie Faracy. Thank God, she said yes. I was at a party at Allee's house and told Michael Patrick King (*Sex and the City*) about my directing debut. He suggested his friend Peter Onorati for the part of the dad, Fran. Peter signed on quickly.

I was so grateful when my casting director friend, Geralyn Flood, offered to help. She had heard that Mindy Sterling was interested in doing theater. I was familiar with Mindy from her career-making role of Frau Farbissina in *Austin Powers*. We set up a time that she could come to the theater while we were holding auditions. I asked her to read with some of the actors, a good way to see how comfortable she was with me and the part of "Lucille," the girlfriend of Peter's character, famously played by Anne DeSalvo in the Broadway production. Anne's TV commercial tag line of "I'll just pick," while scarfing down spaghetti, was legendary in Manhattan in the 80s. Mindy was perfect for the part.

In rehearsal, I really took to directing. I found clever ways to make the play my own. And being detail-oriented, I even had the stage manager cook garlic on a hot plate backstage, then walk around the theater before we opened house for each performance. I wanted the audience to really smell what those old tenements smelled like. Audiences responded. It was so gratifying that I knew I had to do more theater directing.

Another opportunity arose when a producer friend told me he

was looking for a Christmas play to fill a slot at his ninety-nine-seat theatre in Hollywood. I'd always loved *A Tuna Christmas* and thought it would be a perfect fit. It only needed two actors, but they had to play twelve characters each, all residents of Tuna, a tiny Texas town.

The play is usually performed by two men, but I had a vision— Mindy Sterling with a mustache and cowboy hat. I knew she had years of character work with the legendary improv group, the Groundlings. Mindy suggested Patrick Bristow (*Showgirls*), also in the Groundlings. A brilliant pairing, if I must say so myself!

We ended up getting Critic's Choice from the *LA Times* and sold out our run. This cemented the beautiful friendship I was beginning to form with Mindy Sterling. A friendship that was becoming so meaningful to me and made me realize that since I didn't have a relationship or kids of my own, these wonderful actors were becoming my "Chosen Family." How lucky was I to have them all in my life.

12

RITA TO THE RESCUE

I *could stop the book right here.* Be literal with the title. But so much has happened since *Gilmore Girls,* and it certainly isn't the end of my story. Plus, I've met SO many more wonderful women, I must continue . . .

After our stint on *Gilmore Girls,* Jim and I went back into "Development Hell." They call it that because, as you can tell by now, you spend so much time creating shows that never see the light of day. That's why Jim and I decided to start writing our ideas on spec. Which basically means for free. This way we can show them exactly what we see. And hope then they will realize the potential that we do.

One of the spec scripts we were excited about we called *Rita Rocks.* It married our love for domestic sitcoms, like *Roseanne,* and music. I can't tell you how many hours and how much money I spent at Tower Records and the Virgin Megastore back in the day. My music vocabulary grew with each visit as I explored recording artists of every genre and decade. I guess there are worse vices to have. Although I probably could've made more contacts in AA or NA.

Rita Rocks was about a suburban Detroit mom who lost her groove. To help get her identity back, she climbs a ladder in her garage and takes down her old guitar from the rafters. She ultimately starts a band with her Black postal lady, her unemployed next-door neighbor, and her daughter's hot, young boyfriend. Our script was sharp and funny, with a bit of indie film edge. Obviously influenced by all those movies my mom took me to. At one point, Katey Sagal (*Married . . . with Children*) wanted to play Rita. She could've really rocked that part. But then she was advised against it.

It seemed we were met with roadblocks at every turn. Were we washed up in the business? That's how we felt. We got so despondent one day that we pulled over on the Pacific Coast Highway and prayed there'd be an earthquake and boulders from the mountainside would come tumbling down and smash Jim's Range Rover. With us in it! I know, a bit melodramatic.

Right then, his cell phone rang. It was Melissa Myers, one of our agents. She had slipped our *Rita Rocks* script to Lifetime after hearing they wanted to branch out from their women-in-plight TV movies and start producing original sitcoms.

JANUARY 24, 2008   JOURNAL ENTRY

Lifetime wants to make *Rita Rocks*. How incredible is that?! This could be SO cool. They want
Reba McEntire. We'll know on Monday if she's interested. Mindy Schultheis & Michael Hanel are
the execs at our studio, MRC. We've been waiting
a long time for something like this to happen!

We worked with Mindy and Michael when they were comedy development executives during our overall deal at 20th Century Fox. My opinion of them was cemented when, after pitching a show idea, Mindy's comment was, "Can't do it. It's never been done."

That was a reason NOT to do it? We'd often leave their office feeling demoralized. I thought their job was to get their writers excited.

So, I was pleasantly surprised to hear Mindy be so complimentary toward us and our script. I was cautiously optimistic. When Reba passed, we all jumped in and started making lists of possible actors for the title role. My favorite part of the pilot process.

FEBRUARY 18, 2008

Long day of casting. Still no Rita. Lifetime
has been so picky. They passed on our top two
choices, Kristen Johnston and Megan Mullally
(Will & Grace). Both have won multiple Emmys,
and Megan's been in Broadway musicals and
has a band. But they're not good enough for
Lifetime? Insane! Our search continues . . .

Some women who came in to read for us: Rosanna Arquette,
Taylor Dayne, Melissa Gilbert, Heather Paige Kent, Lori Loughlin,
Vicki Lewis, Wendi McClendon-Covey, Holly Robinson Peete, Lea
Thompson . . . super-talented and experienced actors but not right for
one reason or another.

Then I had a brainstorm. What about Paige Davis from the home
improvement show, *Trading Spaces*? I felt she had a Mary Tyler Moore
"Every Woman" quality. She lived in Manhattan, and fortunately I
talked the network into hiring an East Coast casting person. I got
them to fly me there to see Paige and some other possibilities.

FEBRUARY 25, 2008   JOURNAL ENTRY

I'm in NYC. Gonna leave soon to get to my
first day of casting. Please let Paige Davis
be great today. Having Sandra Bernhard audition for me will be a bit odd. I don't want
to waste her time, but she said she wants to
come in for this, and I wanted to give her the
opportunity. The life of an actor . . .

Some of the actors I got to meet on that trip were Carolee
Carmello, Victoria Clark, Renée Elise Goldsberry (pre-*Hamilton*),
Alice Ripley, Claudia Shear (who insisted that Lifetime would never
hire a plus-size lead), Aida Turturro . . .

I even read the two-time Tony Award winner Donna Murphy. In order for her to come in, I had to agree to a half-hour sit-down with her. I was actually looking forward to it since the last time I saw her was waiting in line for some brown Salisbury steak in the Weinstein Hall cafeteria at NYU. She dropped out freshman year to be in the ensemble of the soon-to-be hit Broadway musical, *They're Playing Our Song*. We were all in awe of her sudden success at such a young age. She gave us hope that we could make it as actors. Donna surprised me. Usually she's cast in aristocratic roles (like on *The Gilded Age*), but she played it real. I think people underestimate her. And we knew she could sing her ass off. Unfortunately, Lifetime didn't see it. Really?!

Sandra was really good too. She took it seriously, and I was impressed. As I was with Paige. I'd never seen her act before, and she came off exactly like I thought, completely loveable. Lifetime wouldn't even consider Sandra.

I was growing frustrated. With time running out, I strongly suggested Paige be flown to LA for the network test. The network and studio had major discussions about it but ultimately didn't like that she was on a show on another network and wouldn't make the deal.

Cyndi Lauper really wanted the part too. She'd won an Emmy for her guest star role on *Mad About You* and would be a real "get." We'd have to rewrite the part for her and probably set it in a new location, like New Jersey. But it was Cyndi Lauper! Superstar and an awesome singer/songwriter. If you've never been to one of her live concerts—RUN! She throws herself into every performance. It's a wonder to behold.

---

*QUICK SIDEBAR

I'd met Cyndi a few years earlier when she was making an album with Allee Willis and staying at her house. Allee called me to come babysit Cyndi. I was more than happy to. That night we all went downtown to see the Pet Shop Boys perform. Allee had written "What Have I

Done to Deserve This?" with them. When we got
to the front entrance, the bouncer asked to
see Cyndi's ID before he would let her in.
I couldn't believe what I was hearing and
very strongly told him, "SHE'S FUCKING CYNDI
LAUPER!" He let us in.

Cyndi was about to head to Australia to promote her new album, and Lifetime wasn't willing to postpone our pilot shoot by a week. Jim and I were not happy. Couldn't they see how huge this would be?! We were forced to keep looking.

In the end, we took three actors to the network for the part of Rita—Nicole Sullivan (*Mad TV*), Beth Littleford, and our old friend, Charlotte Ross. Nicole got the part. She's an EXTREMELY skilled comedienne. She has a way of enveloping each line and giving it so many layers. Like petals on a flower.

As Patty Mannix, Rita's Black mail carrier, we brought Jasmine Guy (*A Different World*), Tisha Campbell-Martin (*Martin*), and Octavia Spencer (pre-Oscar for *The Help*) to the network. How do you pick from that illustrious trio? Unfortunately, Octavia said she couldn't sing. But she sure was funny. And one of the nicest people in the business. To this day, if I email her, I hear back within a half hour. Who does that?! Very impressive.

So, it was really between Jasmine and Tisha. The network strongly urged us to pick Tisha, feeling she came off more likable. That's important to a network. And Tisha certainly sparkles. She got the part.

MARCH 31, 2008   JOURNAL ENTRY

Such an exhausting time making our pilot. We
didn't leave the studio until 3 a.m. I only
had two hours of sleep because we had to be
back for a table read/rehearsal at 8 a.m. That
night, after the run-through, the network told

us to come up with an entirely new B-story
line about parenting. At this late date! I
didn't freak. Just went right into "fix it"
mode. We pulled twelve hour days and wrote an
amazing new script. All went well on Monday.
We shot it on Wednesday. At first the network
and Mindy & Michael were all over us on set,
giving us nonstop notes. But then they didn't
leave their chairs. I think they saw that
Jim, Andrew Weyman (our director), and I had
it under control. The cast instantly gelled,
like they'd been doing this show for years.
Everyone could see that. Susanne Daniels,
Lifetime's President, supposedly "high-fived"
people upstairs in the Green Room. If this
doesn't get picked up to series, I'd be really
surprised. It's SO perfect for Lifetime.

Our pilot tested great with focus groups in Atlanta and Chicago.
We were able to watch it live via satellite. I was shocked when one
woman objected to the daughter character using the word "vagina."
She said she doesn't even say that word to her doctor. I told the network we are NOT taking out the word based on one woman's opinion.
And if you can't say that word on Lifetime, you might as well take it
out of the dictionary. It stayed in. One big lesson I've learned over the
years is—"Pick your battles." I had no idea of the battle that was about
to come our way.

MAY 12, 2008   JOURNAL ENTRY

Susanne Daniels is insisting that a condi-
tion of the network picking up our pilot to
series is that we must bring on experienced
executive producer/writers. Not co-showrun-
ners, but OVER us. "Mommy" writers. Because
two gay men couldn't possibly run a show about

a working mom. I'm insulted and speechless.
She said something about not feeling confident
with us. I think she's using that as an excuse
so we can't sue. I want to. Jim doesn't. I'm
ticked off at our lawyer for not sticking up
for us. After how hard we worked and what a
great pilot we made. Our agent Paul Haas went
ballistic. But Susanne is being stubborn.

Susanne Daniels not only wanted to bring writers on over us, she
had a specific writing team—Jeffrey Hodes and Nastaran Dibai. A
married couple with a kid who had worked on *The Nanny* for a billion
years. We told the network we had always planned on hiring a staff
with as many female writers as possible. But Susanne wouldn't budge.
It was Hodes & Dibai, or no show. We agreed to meet with them. They
picked the Avalon Hotel on Pico.

MAY 14, 2008   JOURNAL ENTRY

Had trouble sleeping last night. I don't understand why Susanne Daniels is doing this.
That seems to be a theme in my life. Figuring
out the "why." Maybe I have to accept things at
face value. That's what my therapist thinks.
Like my parents' divorce, or why Jim wouldn't
do the Bravo show, or why I can't find love.

We met Hodes & Dibai. It was awkward. For all
of us. But we felt we had no choice but to say
yes to them, even though a few friends said
to walk away from the show entirely. We didn't
take their advice. Rita Rocks was "officially"
picked up.

JUNE 2, 2008   JOURNAL ENTRY

The thought of Hodes & Dibai taking over
our show is really haunting me. I can't believe Jeffrey Hodes said he'd "listen" to our
thoughts. Just listen?! That hurts! It's so
hard to go into this with a positive attitude.
What lesson is this? Please help me with it.
I've got to find peace with it. I've got to!!

JUNE 23, 2008   JOURNAL ENTRY

The first day of *Rita Rocks.* Susanne Daniels
resigned from Lifetime. Or was fired. Doesn't
matter. She's out of my life. Thank you for
listening, up there! Hodes & Dibai got into a
huge fight with the network and actually hung
up on them. Jeffrey told them the phone got
disconnected. I have to remember to stay above
it all. It will shake out the way it's meant
to. At least I don't have to see Susanne at our
first table read! I don't know if I could've
been nice to her face.

JUNE 28, 2008   JOURNAL ENTRY

Week one at *Rita.* Thank God, I scheduled my
monthly check-in with my therapist. I guess I
needed another life lesson—no matter how good
I am, people do fucked up things. And I may
never get an explanation or be able to understand them. I have to find a way to live with
that. He also clued into Susanne being married to a successful writer, Greg Daniels (The
Office). You'd think she'd be extra sensitive
about writers' feelings. It seems to be the
opposite. Wonder what's going on there? But
that's for her and her therapist to figure out.

In the writers' room, I've started to speak
up more. And will continue to do so. We had
drinks with our Lifetime execs, Maria Grosso
and Julia Gunn. Maria commented on how you can
tell a lot about a person by the way they act
in a crisis. She said, "You guys are handling
yourselves with such class." I will continue
to do that.

JULY 13, 2008   JOURNAL ENTRY

I have to keep reminding myself not to get
pulled into all the work drama. Which seems
to be constant. Just relax and trust I'll know
the right thing to say and do. It's been such
a learning curve. Especially about myself.

I felt kind of bad for Hodes & Dibai. I knew Jeffrey was going
through some major health issues, and that must affect their home
and work life. And I could see they were also struggling with trying to
understand why Lifetime hired them in the first place. Especially since
the network kept telling them to make the series like the pilot Jim and
I made. We didn't understand either. But I don't think they handled it
in the best way from the start.

When Jim and I have been brought in to supervise other writers,
we always went in with the attitude that we were there to help bring
out the creators' voice since it's *their* show. I don't think we were afford-
ed that same courtesy.

In an effort to create a more fun atmosphere on set, we imple-
mented a dance party every Friday after taping. I had our line producer
set up a bar onstage, and Raviv Ullman (an actor in the show) and I
would DJ. We'd spin records, actual LPs. People were shocked when
they saw me and Nastran on the dance floor together. Building unity
was important to me. And there was a side to her I really liked.

Jim and I spent ten years with this script in development, and we had vowed if we ever got another show on the air, we'd do it with love. We felt that the people at the top set the tone. How did it get to a place of such dysfunction on *Rita Rocks*? We were hoping to avoid that after our experiences on *Golden Girls* and *Roseanne*.

One bright spot was getting to meet and work with some really cool female guest stars, like Melissa Peterman. She knew Mindy & Michael from her scene-stealing role of Barbara Jean on the WB sitcom *Reba*. She agreed to do a guest spot. She is one funny lady. I instantly fell in love with her. So talented and quick with a joke suggestion. I told her, "I want to bring you on staff as a punch up writer."

Having our own show was exciting because we got to make a wish list of actors to cast and then actually hire some, like 80s pop star Debbie Gibson and old coworkers like Jennifer Elise Cox and Melissa McCarthy.

Melissa guest starring came about because I was visiting my good friend Alan Poul, who was directing the Jennifer Lopez comedy film, *The Backup Plan*, on the Radford lot where we shot *Rita Rocks*. I had no idea Melissa had a small role in the movie.

When she saw me and found out what Jim and I were up to, she said, "Write me a part!"

I went back to the writers' room and said we had to create a part specifically for her. We came up with a story about a married couple that Rita and her husband befriend when their kids become friends at school. A "parenting" story, so Lifetime was happy. We cast Melissa and Mike McDonald (*Mad TV*), a good friend of Nicole's.

We were all surprised when we went down on Tuesday for the studio run-through. Melissa seemed to just walk through the scenes. Same thing on Wednesday at the network run-through. The staff wanted me and Jim to fire her. Mind you, this was before *Bridesmaids*, so they basically thought she was some actress friend of ours from *Gilmore Girls*.

I didn't understand why Melissa wasn't giving it her all. We all knew how hysterically funny she could be. And she was in the Groundlings improv troupe. To put more pressure on me, my friend Peter Golden, head of casting at CBS, called and asked how she was doing, since she was up for the lead in a new sitcom pilot. I had to be honest. But I said that maybe since she had never done a multi-cam show before, she might not know that you have to give 110 percent for every rehearsal, or you could be let go in an instant.

I stood my ground on keeping Melissa, secretly crossing my fingers and hoping I wouldn't look like a fool on Friday, our "tape night." In front of the studio audience, Melissa came alive. She and Michael were outrageously brilliant. Once we got takes of the lines as written, we said they should go wild and improvise anything they liked. And wild they went, with Nicole going toe-to-toe with them. It was so much fun to watch, but most of it was pretty racy and could never be aired on basic cable. I was relieved to report back to Peter that they should definitely hire Melissa for *Mike & Molly*. Wonder whatever became of her . . . hmmm.

OCTOBER 19, 2008   JOURNAL ENTRY

Nicole and Jeffrey got into a huge fight. Jeffrey refused to go to run-through. Then, in the middle of our shoot week, Jeffrey and Nastaran suddenly leave town to see their daughter in Oregon. We were put in charge to run the show. Jim and I totally stepped up to the plate. We didn't discuss how to do it. We just did it. I don't know how we're going to go back to the old way on Monday when H&D return.

NOVEMBER 16, 2008   JOURNAL ENTRY

Good news! We got picked up for the back seven episodes! H&D are staying. But probably not for the second season if we get picked up.

MARCH 2, 2009   JOURNAL ENTRY

Rita Rocks got picked up for a second season—
twenty episodes! Unbelievable! Hodes & Dibai
will not be running it. We will! They'll be
back, but only as consultants. Some big obsta-
cles this year—two actors are pregnant (Nicole
AND Tisha), and we lost Ian Gomez to another
series, ABC's *Cougar Town*. But we've got to
turn those into positives. Challenge us to be
better. My personal life will have to be put on
hold once again. This is worth it. Here we go!

Get this. Lifetime would not allow two pregnancies with our characters. They thought it would seem too unrealistic. BUT IT HAPPENED IN REAL LIFE!

I came up with the idea that Rita would be pregnant, since that could give us interesting storylines. Now that she finally has her band together, she has this new complication in her life. For Patty, we decided Tisha's character started overeating out of anxiety that her only son was leaving the nest for college next year.

We didn't know how either actor would handle their pregnancies in real life, so I suggested bringing in a new character, Rita's mother, for a multi-episode arc. I thought this could ease the workload and give pages of dialogue to another actor instead of to our two leading ladies. Everybody liked that idea.

We started making a list of actors for the role of Rita's mom. Women from 50 to 70 years old were considered. We even got serious and offered the part to Roseanne. She almost accepted, but then at the last minute, she passed. That would've been a trip, but if her past (and present) is any indication, it would've also been a headache we didn't need.

We then set our sights on Swoosie Kurtz. She became a huge Broadway star when I was a young theater student at NYU. And early in our career we had written that spec script for her NBC series, *Love,*

Sidney. We were told she was interested but wanted to talk to the producers on the phone about her character since there were no pages to read yet. A call was arranged.

```
*FUNNY SIDEBAR
Years ago, Jim and I went to the opening of
Private Lives, starring Richard Burton and
Elizabeth Taylor. I'll never forget Liz walk-
ing in to wild applause. Some queen was running
around yelling at the guests—"Clap for Liz!
Clap for Liz!" Everyone obeyed. Liz looked
like she was floating on air, her feet bare-
ly touching the ground. Later that night, I
happened to start a conversation with a man
in uniform. It was Colonel Kurtz, Swoosie's
father. When he found out Jim and I were writ-
ers, he pulled out his card and said we should
call him because his daughter was an actress,
and we needed to write for her. I never let on
that I knew EXACTLY who his daughter was but
promised him one day I'd make that happen. I
loved that he was pimping her out.
```

Toward the end of our call with Swoosie, I told her that story and said I'd been waiting years to fulfill that promise to her father, who had recently passed. She said yes.

Watching her on set was a master class in acting. And I made sure everyone treated her like the goddess she is. I even told every crew member how to correctly pronounce her name (it's Swoo-see), which she said most people have trouble with. I took great pride when she whispered to me how this was the first show she had been on where everyone said her name properly.

She even invited me to be her date for an event honoring her friend and stage costar Cherry Jones (*Doubt*). In the limo ride to the gala, we had an amazing conversation.

Swoosie: "I'm in awe of you and Jim. How do you do it? Produce such quality scripts on a sitcom, week after week?"

Me: "I'm in awe of *you!* And all your many performances I had the privilege of seeing over the years."

She recounted a story about the Lincoln Center production of *House of Blue Leaves,* which I saw. She said she couldn't figure out her character until right before Opening Night. She went on to win a Tony Award for that role.

I told her about the philosophy Jim and I used. Early on, we decided to *take fear off the table.* We didn't want to live in that negative space and had grown to trust that we'd figure it out. In the end, we knew we'd always have a great script. That thinking has saved me years of anguish. And probably lots of gray hairs too. I think that's one of the reasons people feel this sense of calm around me. And how much love and heart I put into every project. That limo ride was magical, as is every minute I spend with Swoosie.

JANUARY 5, 2010   JOURNAL ENTRY

Mindy and Michael called to say Rita is not being renewed for a third season. What will become of us? I feel SO grateful for the experience. But I can't help thinking about all those people out of jobs. That's what my mom would notice when she comes down from Santa Barbara for the tapings. We were in charge of so many people on set. I will miss them all. Well, most of them. Doors opening, doors closing, as spiritual guru, Louise Hay would say. I must mourn now. But I'm also excited about the future. I know my talents will be put to good use.

And they were. I dove headfirst, back to my first love, where I always feel at home—LIVE THEATER.

13

BACK ON THE BOARDS

A*n idea I had for many years* was a theater musical play using TV theme show songs. I thought the possibilities of this were endless—Off Broadway, regional companies, community theater, high schools, even cruise ships. I pitched it to Jim over and over, but he just didn't see it.

I finally found someone who did: Christian McLaughlin. I knew Christian and his writing partner, Valerie Ahern, from their work on such shows as *Married . . . with Children* and *Desperate Housewives*. Christian helped punch up jokes on *Situation: Comedy* and *Rita Rocks*. We decided to write the piece as a jukebox musical using over forty theme songs—everything from *I Love Lucy* to *The Big Bang Theory*. We called it "It's On!" Growing up, I was like a human TiVo. I'd decide which program was suitable for each family member and when their appropriate show was about to air, I'd yell, "IT'S ON!"

Once we completed a first draft, the next step was assembling a reading in my living room. Naturally, there was a part for Mindy Sterling. Tisha Campbell agreed to read the role of "Whitney Thomas-Harris," a diva sessions singer of TV theme songs. The leads were a male/female songwriting team who were in love but never admitted it to each other. I cast the guy, but needed the girl.

As fate would have it, I was at the valet stand in the parking lot at Vermont, a supper club in Los Feliz, with producer Janet Billig

Rich. Out of the corner of my eye, I saw a lot of blonde hair and a million-dollar smile. I realized it was Megan Hilty, whom I had seen in the musical *Nine to Five*. I don't know where I got the nerve, but I marched over to her, probably threw out my *Golden Girls* credit, spit out my elevator pitch of the show, and asked her if she'd be up to do a reading of it at my house. Shockingly, she said yes!

The reading went so well, Janet arranged for a twenty-nine-hour Equity workshop at Garry Marshall's theater in Toluca Lake. Tisha was unavailable, but Sheryl Lee Ralph (*Dreamgirls* and now Emmy winner for *Abbott Elementary*) was. Sheryl Lee Ralph is otherworldly. I would do anything for her. And have.

---

*QUICK SIDEBAR

For two years, Christian and I wrote the scripts for Sheryl Lee's annual DIVAS: SIMPLY SINGING! AIDS benefits. It's a simple format: each diva sings one song, then leaves the stage. In between, Sheryl Lee does some funny patter. Our first year, I was over the moon when I learned there would be a *Dreamgirls* reunion with the original three leading ladies—Sheryl Lee, Loretta Devine, and Jennifer Holliday. *Dreamgirls* was the last Broadway show I saw before moving to LA. Standing room for fifteen dollars. It was all I could afford. And lucky to get that since it had just opened and taken Broadway by storm.

Since Jennifer's character, "Effie," famously ended Act One with the showstopping "And I'm Telling You . . .," we decided to end our Act One that way as well. But literally during the show, Jennifer said she wasn't ready with her hair and makeup. And she decided that she didn't want to sing with the other two women, only do her famous song solo. Sheryl Lee was

beside herself backstage. I calmed her down
and pitched how we could switch singers around
to end the night with the *Dreamgirls* reunion.
I told her to let Jennifer have the stage to
herself for her song, but before she does,
look her and Loretta in the eye and . . .

Me: "Tell them how much they mean to you. And
how appreciative you are that they come back
to support this benefit year after year. Just
speak from the heart."

She nodded and went off to continue her hosting duties. When it came time for the closing number, Sheryl Lee gathered Loretta and
Jennifer around the piano and started talking
to them. Honestly and with real emotion. The
piano player started to play "We Are a Family"
from *Dreamgirls*, softly in the background.
Suddenly, one by one, the women all started
singing together. Naturally, as if on cue,
sending goosebumps throughout the packed auditorium. A night I'll never forget.

Okay, back to our workshop reading of my TV theme song musical. I finally got to meet the great Garry Marshall. The night before
our first show, I was called to his office. It was kind of like going to see
the Wizard of Oz. I walked down a long hallway, my legs shaking. This
was the man responsible for so many sitcoms I watched growing up.

When I finally entered the inner sanctum, Garry was so warm and
treated me like family. He said he always stands on stage and welcomes
the audience before introducing every show. He wanted me to do that.

Those were big shoes to fill, especially since I knew he'd be watching me from his designated seat in the last row of the theater. I knocked
it out of the park and even engaged him with a joke. It felt great to
make a comedy legend like him laugh. And I didn't have to shoot a

basketball! He was such a mensch, at the matinee, he made a point of walking all the way across the theater to shake my mom's hand.

Garry: "I just had to come over here to meet you and say what a great job you did raising a fine gentleman like Stan."

He was one classy guy.

It's On! went over like gangbusters, like I knew it would. We brought the show to NYMF (New York Musical Theatre Festival) for a special staged reading at the new Signature Theatre. Whoopi Goldberg came to our matinee, having worked with Sheryl Lee Ralph in *Sister Act 2.*

A couple years later, through a connection, I got it to Jimmy Fallon, and his company optioned it. I thought, "Finally. It's with the right person!" Unfortunately, after a close call, it went nowhere. I still have high hopes for it.

I turned my focus back to directing. This time directing work by other playwrights. I received nice notices for an intimate LA production of Theresa Rebeck's *Spike Heels,* then helmed Joe Orton's *Entertaining Mr. Sloane.* I was able to attach a killer company. Casting against type, I had Olivia d'Abo in a frumpy, unglamorous part. I immersed myself in the world and music of 60s London. We got glowing notices and became a buzz in town. We even started attracting paparazzi to our stage door. I felt like I was on working on Broadway. And desperately wanted to be.

On one of my many visits to New York, while nursing a martini, theater producer Larry Hirschhorn told me, "Stop directing other people's plays. You're a writer. Write your own. About you!"

I scoffed, "Who would want to see a play about my life?"

Later that night, a light bulb went off. I had an idea for my first play. I texted Christian, who responded that he thought it was brilliant. (Why do martinis always seem to be involved at major turning points for me?)

Returning to LA, we started writing *Meet & Greet.* It wasn't exactly my life, but about what I've made actors do all my life—audition for me. The play centers around four actresses of a certain age, who all end up in the waiting room of a major network when they come to audition for a really bad sitcom pilot. Written by men.

Once again, we started with a small reading in my living room. Liking what we heard, I got the play to the Blank Theatre, and they wanted to do a staged reading. They have a crazy policy at the Blank that the writer can't direct their own work, so I asked my friend, Amanda Bearse, to take over. Once again, I was being pushed aside for no good reason, but I knew Amanda understood the world of actors since her days on *All My Children*.

Next step was assembling a stellar ensemble. Carolyn Hennesy, who played Margo, the self-absorbed New York theater vet, was on board from our first house reading. She was literally that role. I loved Vicki Lewis (*NewsRadio*) and begged her to be in it. I think she said yes mainly to shut me up. The always hysterical Kym Whitley (*Curb Your Enthusiasm*) was luckily available for the part of the reality show character who was trying her hand at "actressing." But who would play the blonde, Suzanne Somers type? That was a really tricky role.

One night I was invited to the Magic Castle, and while sitting at the bar, again with a martini, I looked over, and a spotlight hit this beautiful blonde actor that I'd seen on so many sitcoms, game shows, and talk shows. It was Teresa Ganzel. I made my way over to her. The next thing I know, she's at the theater for rehearsals. Teresa is such a gifted actor. I don't understand why she isn't working 365 days a year.

Everything was going great until dress rehearsal. Vicki ran on stage, looked out to the audience, and said, "I think I'm going to be sick!"

Then ran off stage. A few friends in the audience thought it was part of the play. It wasn't. Amanda, ever the trouper, grabbed her script, jumped onstage, and finished the rehearsal in Vicki's role, the Joyce DeWitt type character. Vicki was so sick with food poisoning, she had to go to the hospital. That's how I became director, and Amanda was back on the boards after years in the TV director's chair.

PLEASE KNOW I didn't have anything to do with Vicki's illness. There was no *Showgirls* moment, I swear!

Everyone adored the play, so we signed up for the 2014 Hollywood Fringe Festival. Vicki returned to the role. She came to my house for the first day of rehearsal, not really knowing me or my abilities as a director. She had definite ideas for the character and blocking. I mean, she should, she's been on so many TV shows and Broadway. I asked her to try a physical comedy bit I thought of. She was skeptical but gave it a go.

It worked fantastically, and she said, "I'm going to shut up and do whatever you want me to."

Anyone would be lucky to have a talent like her in their show . . . and life.

Kym Whitley couldn't do our full production, so we got the amazing Danielle Gaither (*Mad TV*). She was also a Groundlings alum and is always game for anything.

It's no wonder it became a huge hit with critics and audiences with that dream cast. In a rarity for LA theater, we managed to run the show for five months to sold-out audiences. I went to every performance. I loved hearing them scream with delight at our lines. Better than any drug. Plus, I wanted to meet all the wonderful actresses who showed up—Edie McClurg, Erin Murphy (Tabitha from my beloved *Bewitched*), Lynne Stewart, Joan Van Ark, Jo Anne Worley, and dear Swoosie Kurtz. Those women knew firsthand the horrors of sitting in a casting office, continually putting themselves on the line for material that was usually dreck.

Everything with *Meet & Greet* was going great. I couldn't wait for my mom to drive down from Santa Barbara and see it. But on the Sunday that she was coming in for a matinee, she didn't arrive at my house when she said she would. I started to worry. I called her cell phone. It went to voice mail. I tried her at home, got the machine. I called Rande and Peter, who did their best to calm me down. It was getting closer to the time I needed to leave for the theater. Finally, my mom picked up her cell phone. She was at a gas station, lost down-town. She missed the exit to get off the 101. An exit she had taken a billion times. I jumped in my car and by some miracle found her. I told her to get in my car, but she was her usual stubborn self and said she'd follow me back to my house in her car. She did. We rushed to the theater barely in time for curtain. I was mad *and* scared.

Next morning, I told her, "We're going to look at Belmont Village Assisted Living. It's literally three minutes from my house, by the Hollywood Bowl. I'm not taking no for an answer."

She didn't fight me.

We took a tour. It was really difficult seeing all the old people there. They didn't look like my mother. She was polite to the Belmont staff, but back in my car, she said she wasn't ready for that. The struggle to get her to move would continue. For years . . .

I noticed on Teresa Ganzel's Facebook page that her NY producer friend, Morgan Sills, commented how much he wished he could see *Meet & Greet*. I posted back that he can—help get us to New York.

Long story short, I sent him the script, he loved it, and we started planning a big backers' reading in Manhattan. We asked Amanda to once again direct. I heard the same thing about the New York theater world, that the playwright shouldn't direct their own work. This atti-tude is prevalent because so many NY playwrights refuse to rewrite. I promised everyone that I wasn't precious about our words, which I'd learned from years as a TV writer, being rewritten on a weekly basis. It fell on deaf ears. But I loved working with Amanda, and we assem-bled another amazing cast that included Teresa, now alongside Rachel Dratch (*SNL*), Isabel Keating (*The Boy from Oz*), Sherri Shepherd (*The View*), and my buddy Michael Urie.

The feedback from our NY reading of *Meet & Greet* was positive, but they wanted some script changes. Christian was having none of that. I think his years of writing on *Jessie*, a Disney Channel show, left him wanting theater to be a place for free expression. Not more note-taking. But that's not realistic. You always have to be open to criticism, especially if people are investing large sums of money in your play.

I said to him, "What's the point of having material stuck on our computers where no one will see it? Plays are meant to be performed."

I could've seen that as a sign to back off working with him again, but I felt I couldn't write by myself. And we created really good work together.

Theater was feeding my soul, but not my pocketbook. I needed a way to make money, and I was also loving directing. Since many people told me I should be directing multi-cam comedies, I decided to use my connections to shadow directors.

For a year, I was able to get on sets of over thirteen sitcoms. On ABC-TV's *Malibu Country*, I got to see my old pal, Lily Tomlin. With *Melissa & Joey*, I tried to buddy up with Melissa Joan Hart. She wasn't into it. Although Joey Lawrence's mom seemed to really like me. On *Two Broke Girls*, I got to hang with Jennifer Coolidge, who kept bugging me for my facial skincare regime. Strangely, after meeting her on set, there was a month when no matter where I went out to dinner, she'd be in the booth next to me. We'd end up sitting together, laughing and drinking wine. She's as funny and wonderful as she seems.

Although I made a lot of new fans on these shows, and everyone said this is what I should be doing, NOT ONE producer offered me an episode. Watching some of these shows, I know I could've done a great job and been wonderful with the actors and the writer/producers, having lived in all those worlds.

But the best part that came out of all that time spent on those sets was connecting with so many new actresses that I didn't know personally. Like the great Wendie Malick (*Just Shoot Me*). She was so warm and the only lady on *Hot in Cleveland* who asked me about myself.

When Christian and I went to write our next play, *Knife to the Heart*, we wrote the mother role specifically for her. *Knife* is a comedy about an interfaith couple who find out they're pregnant. The Jewish boy's mom throws a fit when they question whether to have their twin sons circumcised. It was an honor when Wendie agreed to take part in a few of our readings. Her insight into the script was so valuable to the development of the play. She's the total package—smart, beautiful, and funny as hell.

We were all set to go to Chicago for a backers' reading at the famed Second City, with Chelsea Kane (whom I met shadowing on *Baby Daddy*) joining our Chicago actors. Also, a wonderful person and underrated comedienne. Two days before leaving, Wendie got a TV movie. Stepping in with grace and energy was Marilu Henner, who coincidentally lives down the street from me.

I had so much fun traveling with Marilu back to her hometown for this event. I kept pinching myself, remembering seeing her at a *Taxi* taping when Jim and I first moved to LA. Now she was asking ME for character notes on words I had written. Even at this stage in my career, I was still surprised by the level of actors I was now getting to play with.

When we couldn't find enough backers to bring the play to Chicago, I decided to mount it in LA at the Complex Hollywood. Chelsea wasn't available the dates we needed her, but Andrea Bowen (*Desperate Housewives*) came highly recommended. Andrea was living in NYC, but offered to fly herself out and start rehearsals immediately. A good thing for me because I soon discovered we spoke the same theater language. I barely had to give her direction; she's always instantly on it. And it was great for her because she fell in love with her costar, Josh Zuckerman. Again, people, always say, "Yes, and . . ."

I was excited about our cast, which included the hysterical Todd Sherry, whom I met when he did a guest spot on *Rita Rocks*. Wendie and Marilu were also unavailable, but then Pat Richardson (*Home Improvement*) signed on. As soon as I ordered our marquee banner and postcards, Pat got a movie gig and had to bow out. By that point, I'd learned that with intimate theater in LA, you can't stress. You have to have a "we'll make it work" attitude. And I did. Pat suggested her good friend, Anne DeSalvo (*Gemini*), who jumped in and provided me with another wonderful full-circle moment. We sold out that run and are still hoping for the play to move forward.

My theatrical hot streak continued with our next original play, *Yes, Virginia*, a two-hander (play for two actors) inspired by my mom and Virginia Campbell, my Black housekeeper growing up. I used this piece as a way to process my mother's increasing dementia and our struggle to get her to move out of her Santa Barbara condo.

One day my mother said to me, "Why can't I stay in my home and live with Virginia? We could take care of each other."

I said, "That's a wonderful idea, but unfortunately Virginia died years ago."

On my drive back to LA, I began to think this was a great jumping-off point for a play. So did Christian.

Participating at one of the early readings in my living room were two TV icons, Barbara Bain (*Mission Impossible*) and Marla Gibbs (*The Jeffersons*). I still can't believe I was able to make that happen. I joined forces with one of my *Knife to the Heart* producing partners, Stefani Von Huben, and we decided to present the comedy play in a full production at the Complex in December 2018. Stefani's infectious spirit and can-do attitude is a perfect match for me. I'm SO fortunate to have her in my life.

We knew that my muse, Mindy Sterling, had to play Denise. By this point, if I didn't hire Mindy for a part, she'd mock me endlessly on social media. We found the perfect partner for her in the insanely gifted Arnetia Walker (*Nurses*, a spinoff from *Empty Nest*, which was a spinoff of *Golden Girls*). Mindy and Arnetia were a match made in heaven. They complimented each other perfectly. And oddly, had the same agent, same birthday, and each had one son. The play became a must-see holiday hit.

As you can tell, I loved using my house for readings. I think of them as a kind of salon. I've had some outstanding women sitting in my living room, like Illeana Douglas (*To Die For*) and Christina Ricci (*The Addams Family*) playing "Martha" and "Honey" in Edward Albee's classic play *Who's Afraid of Virginia Woolf.* I did another reading of it a few years later with Sherilyn Fenn (*Twin Peaks* and *Gilmore Girls*) as "Martha." Coincidentally, she played Elizabeth Taylor in a bio TV flick, and Elizabeth Taylor had famously starred as "Martha" in the brilliant movie version of the play. I'm obsessed with this piece and know exactly how I want to direct it. One day . . .

As I started to gain a reputation in the theater, I got asked to direct a few one-person shows. Those have been especially gratifying because I get to use all my skills as a writer/director/producer and therapist. I worked with the talented and generous Susannah Blinkoff on her intimate musical show, *Daughter Of,* about her complicated relationship with her mom, who was also a singer/songwriter—Carol Hall (*Best Little Whorehouse in Texas, Free to Be You & Me*).

The other was *Warm Cheese,* created by Teresa Thome. We had a blast when it ran at United Solo Fest at NYC's famed Theatre Row Theatre. She went on to win Best Script, which I take great pride in.

During this time, I was being offered numerous projects dealing with mothers. I had missed writing those dynamics on *Gilmore Girls.* Speaking of which, I did visit the set at Warner Brothers when they were filming the Netflix reboot. By accident, I posted a pic of the snow, not knowing Amy wanted to keep that visual a secret. Oops. I loved sitting with Lauren in between takes and catching up with her. I also went to the dance scene with Rory and Logan. Amy was really cool and said I was always welcome on set, so I took advantage of that.

The same year the reboot was coming out, I read about an upcoming Gilmore Girls Fan Fest. I connected with Jennie Whitaker who, along with her husband Marcus, was starting a new festival in the small town in Connecticut that inspired Amy to create the show and Stars Hollow. Though they had never run a festival, from the very beginning, they did it with such class and precision and love. Through them, and subsequent festivals over the years, I have reconnected, or in most instances, met a lot of the actors (and behind the scenes talent) from *Gilmore Girls* and been able to work with them on my plays. We, and the fans, have become like a little family. They've shown me unconditional love and support. Especially at some particularly difficult times in my life.

One of those difficult times was actually during the first Fan Fest. The Whitakers had rented this mansion on a lake, thinking Amy and Dan or Lauren might show up at the last minute. That was NOT going to happen. Having watched too many episodes of *The Real World*, I knew the first person in the house got the biggest room. I drove like a fiend to Northern Connecticut from my sister's in Greenwich. Once inside, I threw my luggage on the king-size bed, claiming the insanely huge master suite.

One morning, while enjoying the view of the water from a mountain of pillows in bed, my cell phone rang.

OCTOBER 23, 2016   JOURNAL ENTRY

```
I'm in a state of shock. Julie (Silverman)
Sachse just called. She has colon cancer, may-
be liver as well. Stage four. How could this
be happening? I grew up across the street
from Julie. She's supposed to be my "forever
friend." I told her she's a fighter, and she's
surrounded by so much love that she will get
through this. I hung up. But before I could
catch my breath, my phone rings again. It
was an 805 Santa Barbara number, but not my
mom's. It was her neurologist. He was VERY
concerned about her high blood pressure. He
felt we needed to know more, and when I return
to CA, I should come up and we can talk about
options. Now I have to put on a smile and go
to the festival for my first panel. People are
counting on me.
```

And I did. Even though it was pouring rain (how fitting), you couldn't help but feel the love of the fans and the joy from the cast and

crew upon seeing each other. One of the most special relationships
I've gained from the festivals is the privilege of getting to know Liz
Torres. I was a longtime fan of hers since her days on Norman Lear
and MTM shows. And of course, *The John Larroquette Show*, which
garnered her multiple Emmy nominations.

I "officially" met Liz when I landed in the same karaoke room as
her and Sally Struthers for the *Gilmore Girls* wrap party the year we
were on the show. A party which Amy and Dan refused to attend. Jim
and I begged Amy to come, even offering to pick her up and drive her
home. The event wasn't even fifteen minutes from their house.

We had a great time, regardless. Liz and Sally battling it out in
song was a sight to behold and a treat for the ears.

It wasn't until the first festival in Connecticut that I got a chance
to sit and really talk to Liz. I was a bit intimidated, afraid I couldn't
keep up with her or she wouldn't like me.

Returning to LA after the first festival, I was visiting my mom,
whom we'd finally gotten to move down from Santa Barbara and into
Belmont Village in Hollywood.

I was in the office, and the coordinator said, "Someone you know
just moved in here."

I asked, "Who?"

She said, "I can't tell you. Company policy."

Then why the hell did you bring it up?!

I managed to pry it out of her. It was Liz. Liz didn't have early-on-
set dementia like my mother. But she had issues with mobility, making
it difficult for her to live on her own.

Soon, during my weekly visits with my mom, Liz would sit with
us and share stories. Amazing tales of New York and working at the
Baths with Bette Midler, then coming to Hollywood and appearing
on my favorite variety shows and specials. She also told me that she'd
watch after my mom. I adore Liz. I feel so lucky that *Gilmore Girls* and
my mom brought us together.

The more plays I directed and produced on my own, the more

I felt this newfound confidence in exploring my own artistic voice, without the help of Jim or Christian. I began to wonder if I could write by myself. I'd never attempted it. I enjoyed brainstorming with other like-minded artists.

Then an incident propelled me to take the leap. My good friend Kevin Gill died by suicide. I soon realized there's so much shame around the topic. I wanted to do something about it. But what? I was a comedy writer.

Then it hit me: What if I created a play using real suicide notes, similar to Eve Ensler's interviews for *Vagina Monologues*? I started Googling "suicide notes." There were so many, by the famous and not so famous. I copied and pasted them into a folder on my laptop. Occasionally, I'd print them to read, but I'd get too emotional and have to stop. I was still grappling with why Kevin took his life. And I also wanted to read the note he left his ex-lover that referenced me and a few of his close friends. Finally, a theater producer urged me— okay, forced me—to write a play for the upcoming Hollywood Fringe Festival. Which was only four months away!

I convinced myself that I wasn't writing; I was merely curating the notes. I decided my cast would be two men and two women. Two older, two younger.

The reaction to this piece was overwhelming and a start to a much-needed conversation. A conversation that was incredibly personal to me, not only because of Kevin, but because of all the feelings I had struggling as a teenager to accept who I really was.

I connected with the general manager of *It's On!* when we performed it at NYMF in NYC. She had a friend who had died like Kevin. She read the play and eventually optioned it. She brought in Broadway director Michael Wilson, and we all began working on the piece, renaming it *right before I go*.

A huge benefit was planned for NYC's Town Hall in December of 2017. The list of actors was insane, including Elizabeth Ashley, Ellen Burstyn, Hari Nef, Alice Ripley, and as host for the evening, Vanessa

Williams. God bless Judith Light. She got a movie role but didn't want to miss out on the evening, so they filmed her assigned suicide note. She is so giving of her time and talent. You won't find one person to say a bad word about her.

DECEMBER 3, 2017   JOURNAL ENTRY

After instructing me to remain silent in an
email, Michael Wilson really looked to me
in rehearsal. I got to give acting notes to
Academy Award winner Ellen Burstyn, about
Virginia Woolf's suicide note. I was shocked
that I became so emotional when I showed the
cast Kevin's picture. It's still so raw. What
we're doing is extremely powerful and could
change the landscape of the discussion. I
feel I'm at the start of something major. The
Broadway community has taken a real liking to
our production and seems quite impressed.

DECEMBER 4, 2017   JOURNAL ENTRY

It's the day after our "RBIG" Town Hall benefit. I cried many times on the walk over to
the theater. I didn't see the seedy side of
Times Square. I was too in awe of how far I had
come from the scared NYU student dreaming of
one day working with such luminaries. I need
to breathe and process. I have many thoughts
about the direction, production, actors, etc.
That's for another day. Today is to celebrate
a dream come true. And the beginning of a long
(and fruitful) journey with this play.

The evening never could've happened without the generous support of Diane Orley, who lost her son to suicide. I was introduced
to this special human by my friend Julie Sachse who, even though

her cancer had progressed, managed to fly to NYC from LA to be at Town Hall. Weak as she was, she was NOT going to miss that event. Especially since she had been involved in the early days of me making up plays in my basement as a kid.

Although the show was a huge success, Michael Wilson and I kept tinkering with it.

He wondered, "Instead of just facts and suicide notes, is there a way for you to infuse the piece with your personal story with Kevin? The way you talk about him and life will add humanity and much-needed humor."

I thought about it and started working on a "Narrator" character, but it would NOT be me. I was afraid to write by myself, but also to open my heart. It was too painful to relive all the emotions I felt about losing such a close friend.

But I pushed through. I had to. The spine of the play eventually became a story about what happens to a funny person when something tragic happens in their life. Not knowing anything about suicide, I did what most people do when they're ignorant about a subject—they turn on their computer and start to Google. That's how the notes now organically pop up in the play. I still kept the concept of a small ensemble reading all the notes and facts.

This new version was set for Orlando, Florida, on Suicide Prevention Day. My sole request to Michael Wilson was to cast someone older and funny as the "Narrator." He did, but the actor got a paying gig and dropped out at the last minute.

Michael pointed to me, "You're up, kid."

We sat around a table to read it out loud for the first time. When I got to the part where I had to say Kevin's name, it got stuck in my throat. I felt if I said it, tears would come gushing out, and I wouldn't be able to stop. Mindy Sterling was there and grabbed my wrist with a reassuring hold. I pushed through as my glasses filled with tears. The same thing happened that night at the show. It was tough for me, but made for a compelling performance.

I've been lucky to continue acting in the piece, returning to the stage where I feel most at home. During Covid, we did a virtual version; this time I had to act opposite Vanessa Williams. She's looking all gorgeous. I mean, how could she not? And I'm there with my $45 ring light. Not intimidating at all.

Krista Carson Elhai, the drama teacher at Claremont High School in Southern California, also asked me to perform it. She had read about our benefit at Town Hall and tracked me down online. God bless the internet.

This time I'd be sharing the stage with twenty-five people: students, teachers, and school board members. Many moments stand out for me in Claremont, but one is the strongest. A young female actor/student came up and wanted to walk me backstage to return my microphone.

Me: "Thanks, but I think I remember how to get back there."

She insisted, "No. I want to show you the way."

On our walk there, she admitted, "I haven't really told anyone here at school, but I'm a cutter. That's why being a part of your play has really helped me heal."

I wasn't prepared for that reaction. Nor did I realize how coming to Claremont would dramatically alter my life. I kept up a relationship with Krista over the years and told her my goal to have the play licensed so that it could raise money and awareness for suicide. She offered to show it to a few friends at some NY-based theatre licensing companies.

APRIL 14, 2021   JOURNAL ENTRY

Today my life changed. I felt a shift the minute I got off a Zoom call with the team at TRW (Theatrical Rights Worldwide). They said they wanted to rep me and my plays. License and publish them. Starting with *right before I go* and *Yes, Virginia*. This is everything I ever dreamed of. Not my own TV network, but maybe even better. Especially after attempting to claw my way to a New York production. Thinking that was the only way my plays would ever get licensed.

A few years earlier, my mother would've been my first call. Now, with her dementia increasing, I'll wait to tell her in person during our next Monday visit. I almost started crying when I told Rande what just happened. She knows how hard I've been working. And for how long. Could this really be it?! Could I finally be able to breathe? Enjoy the world around me and not just constantly be working? I'm so proud of my tenacity, to keep creating in a world of "No's." As I said to Peter, "Could Allee, Kevin, and Julie (who passed six months ago) have orchestrated this from above?"

I was loving my new life in the theater as opposed to banging my head against closed doors in television and film. I decided to direct and produce the works of playwrights I'd long admired. One was Justin Tanner, a highly respected writer in the LA theater community. Jim and I discovered his quirky plays in the 90s. We'd go see every new one, usually stoned. Which made sense since one of them was called *Pot Mom*, starring a young Laurie Metcalf. We took Amy Sherman to it, and she ended up bringing Justin on staff for *Gilmore Girls*. He lasted one season. He always directs his own plays, so I was surprised when he let me do a revival of his female ensemble comedy, *Heartbreak Help*.

I put together a powerhouse cast, including Melissa Peterman, Sarah Gilman, my secret weapon Teresa Ganzel, and I somehow managed to talk Tony Award winner Marissa Jaret Winokur (*Hairspray*) into making her non-musical theater debut. And at a fifty-seat theater.

The show did not go on without a few bumps along the way. I definitely had PTSD whenever the ladies said they needed to talk to me. They kept asking me to rewrite lines. I wanted to honor Justin's work, which I had seen back in 1996. Surprisingly, Justin encouraged me to do any rewriting I wanted. I was nervous the night he came to the theater, bringing about two dozen of his closest friends. They roared at every line. As did audiences and critics. I received some of my best reviews. Another sold-out show on my hands.

As usual, my mom came to the first Sunday matinee. Doing a play wasn't complete until she showed up. We had such a special relationship. In fact, she once said to me, "If you weren't my son, I'd still want to be your friend."

But that gleam in her eye that I remember growing up had begun to diminish. It was like someone slowly lowering a light with a dimmer. Where was the woman with such spunk and intelligence? She was always there for me, in person or on the other end of a phone. My rock. I wanted that Susanne back. For one day. Or even an hour. But seeing her sit in the front row, so full of pride, was everything. She especially liked the fuss the actors would make over her after the show.

I was having quite a streak with my plays in LA and pondering my next theatrical adventure. I knew I couldn't direct just anything. I awoke in the middle of the night, turned on the TV, and suddenly found my inspiration. I was shocked by a CNN report about a Jewish woman in LA who was hiding a Latinx mom and her daughters when the mom's husband was suddenly deported by ICE.

I sat up in bed and thought, *Are we literally living in the times of Anne Frank?* And then it came to me. What if I directed *The Diary of Anne Frank*, not change a word of the script, but cast everyone in the attic with Latinx actors? The hairs on my arm stood up. Was this a stroke of genius, or was I just having a stroke? (Now I sound like Carrie Bradshaw.)

I waited until the sun rose, then called a few friends who shared my frustration with how the Trump administration was separating children at the border. They all said I had to drop everything and do this play immediately. A big undertaking. I would need ten cast members. I enlisted the brilliant casting director, Julie Gale, and we began looking for actors. I could never have done the play if we hadn't found our Anne, fifteen-year-old Genesis Ochoa.

During our last callback, I asked her, "What grade did you read Anne's diary?"

She said, "To be honest, I didn't know who Anne Frank was until I got the audition."

Smoke practically came out my ears, realizing that the diary is no longer required reading in California schools. I knew then and there that this had become more than a play—it was a cause. And I was determined to get as many student groups in the theater as possible.

The entire cast bonded quickly when, during our first week together, I got a text saying I was trending on Breitbart and Drudge Report, two ultra-right-wing websites. I checked my phone. This "liberal Jewish Hollywood writer" was being accused of changing the Nazis in the script to ICE agents. That wasn't true. I wasn't allowed to change the dialogue and didn't want to. But that didn't stop the story from spreading worldwide.

First, the theater got death threats and was forced to remove our poster from the marquee. Then the licensing house pulled the rights, believing news reports that we were changing the scripts. I had to get my friend Amy Nederlander involved. She produced the Natalie Portman version of the Broadway play we were using. She enlisted her co-producer David Stone and even their director, James Lapine. With those theater heavy hitters involved, the licensing company quickly backed down.

Then, even some of my Jewish friends were wondering why I'd mess with Anne Frank's story. All this without seeing our production. My take was that these Latinx actors were literally putting their feet into the characters' shoes to see how they felt.

I was fortunate to go on *CNN Newsroom with Brooke Baldwin* to explain the truth. When we finally opened, people saw what I was saying with my unique interpretation of the play. I directed it so you felt each character's humanity but also found the humor in being stuck with total strangers for so long. My stark staging of the ending hit audience members in the gut, and they left the theater in tears.

Our school performances were probably the most rewarding. The production went on to play multiple venues, including a Jewish theater festival in Vancouver. I think this has been my most artistic production, as I was able to use lights, music, and colors of costumes to paint my vision. I had no money to buy real sets or costumes. I had to get creative. I don't want Anne's story, or the Holocaust, to die with the few remaining survivors.

As much as I loved making theater, I did miss writing for television. There are so many pluses working in that medium. The first being that you can reach so many more people. That's why Jim and I never gave up creating pilots. Just like Leonard Finger had taught me a million years ago as his assistant in New York, I just had to find new ways to get them produced.

After we wrote *Skirtchasers*, a single-cam, half hour, spec pilot about an estranged relationship between a father and his lesbian daughter, we got very positive feedback. Everyone loved the smart dialogue and said they had never seen a relationship like that on television. One big problem. The networks had already bought their one LGBTQ comedy for the year. Yep, that's right. You can have multiple crime shows or CSIs, but God forbid there would be TWO shows with a gay lead.

Then a savior came to the rescue. Actually two—Elizabeth Keener and Christin Baker. I had been friends with Elizabeth for years through Peter Golden. Elizabeth had made a name for herself as Dawn Denbo on Showtime's *The L Word,* and through that show had gotten to know Christin, who owned Tello Films, the only lesbian content website. Keener, as we call her, sent Christin our *Skirtchasers* script.

During a Sunday afternoon call, Christin casually said, "Let's do it."

We talked a little bit more and then hung up. I called her right back and said, "Did you just greenlight the project?"

She had. I was used to dealing with networks and studios that required a slew of people to sign off on a project. Here she was telling me to go make the script as I saw it. Just do it within her budget, only $25,000.

My next call was to Amanda Bearse, one of the first out lesbians in Hollywood. I asked her to direct four of the webisodes; I'd do the other two. Jim and I cut our half hour script into six pieces. With that low a budget, I was surprised we were able to get the tremendously talented Barry Bostwick (*Rocky Horror Picture Show*) as the father, and a gay icon in her own right, Meredith Baxter (*Family Ties*) as Barry's ex-wife and Elizabeth's mom.

---

*FUN FACT

My parents took me as a kid to see Meredith in *Guys and Dolls* at the Star Theatre in Flint, Michigan. When Meredith arrived at my house for our first table read of *Skirtchasers*, I could tell she was a bit reserved. Not cold, but definitely not warm and fuzzy. I had a surprise for her. I pulled out the *Guys and Dolls* program she'd signed for me as a kid and showed it to her. I told her I've been dying to work with her since she captivated my heart as Sara Brown. She lit up and couldn't have been nicer from that moment on.

Amanda and I came up with the idea of doing a jazzy cover of the 1956 classic song, "Standing on the Corner" as our theme song. The amazingly generous Lea DeLaria offered to record the song and only asked us to pay for her musicians and time in the recording studio. Love. Her.

Christin and I had such a fun time working together, she asked me to do another project with Tello Films. This time, she wanted me to direct all the episodes. I pitched her a bunch of half hour scripts I had in my online trunk. She responded to *Secs & Execs*, which Jim and

I had written for *Lifetime* years ago. It was actually two separate half hours examining the relationships between bosses and their assistants. But in a *Rashomon* kind of way, each half hour from different POVs.

In *Secs*, the assistants were the lead characters, and the bosses were the supporting ones. In *Execs*, it was the opposite. And each show would take place during the same time period. A complicated, but fascinating premise. Jim and I took the best of each script and tightened the material to six webisodes. It was almost better to go back and forth between viewpoints, rather than wait until one half hour was over. I called Julie Gale to cast. We started with actors from the Zimmerman Stable of Stars—Olivia d'Abo, Mindy Sterling, Natalie Dreyfuss and Bayne Gibby (both from *Rita Rocks*), and Sandra Bernhard in a cameo role.

JULY 25, 2016   JOURNAL ENTRY

We start filming *Secs & Execs* a week from tomorrow. I've done most of my blocking prep. Will do a shot list this weekend. I hope Sandra is pleasant to work with. It's been a while since I've seen her.

We paid for an Uber to get Sandra up to my house, where we were filming her two office scenes. I didn't know what to expect. I shot her scenes quickly and efficiently while also getting her to give me choices in editing. She was having such a good time, she didn't want to leave. We hung out in my spare bedroom and chatted like old friends.

The rest of filming went well. I felt Christin and I had a great working relationship. And we loved to strategize. Especially how to promote the show. Although we'd be going up against major companies in the ever-growing web series world, we decided to submit the project to the TV Academy for award season. It would be a David and Goliath type of competition, but we weren't going to let that stop us.

JULY 25, 2017   JOURNAL ENTRY

Just heard the news—Mindy Sterling got nominated for a friggin' Emmy Award for Secs &
Execs. This is HUGE!!!

It was so cool to play dress-up in a tux and go to the Emmys. We sat in the second row, right behind Jane Lynch. Unfortunately, Mindy lost to Jane. Mindy actually got two nominations and probably split her vote. But I fully know how fortunate we are to have found each other. I constantly thank Geralyn Flood for making that happen.

I'm sure by now you realize that I'm the "Gay Kevin Bacon." Mention an actress, and I'm sure they have some connection to me. And writing for all of those wonderful women (yes, even Roseanne) has made me a better man.

14

AND THEN THIS HAPPENED

I *thought my book was going to end there.* But life has a way of throwing you curveballs. I wasn't expecting this one, even though I should have been.

MAY 23, 2021   JOURNAL ENTRY

At 5:35 p.m. PST, my phone rang. Belmont Village Senior Living. There's always fear answering the phone when that number pops up on my caller ID.

Around 5 p.m., my mom was eating dinner, and her tablemate noticed she wasn't talking. Then started drooling on the right side of her mouth. They couldn't understand what she was saying. They called 911 and rushed her to Providence St. Joseph Medical Center in Burbank. She had a stroke. They were putting her on a drug to break up a blood clot in her brain. If that didn't work, they wanted to know how aggressive we wanted to get with saving her. My mom had signed a directive. She didn't want any feeding tubes. I knew that.

I headed to the hospital, where my nephew met me. Cheryl, the day nurse, warned us that my mom had been thrashing about a bit. But she had mobility in all her limbs. I read that as a good sign. I got to see her for a few minutes. That was hard. She took my hand. I told her I loved her, and she was going to be okay, but she needed to rest. She mumbled a bunch of gibberish, but I definitely heard her say, "No!" Not sure what she meant. It's all so much to process.

The night nurse said, "The next twenty-four to thirty-six hours is crucial. We have no idea what the damage is yet."

I'm so worried she won't be able to speak. And after reading about strokes online when I got home, I saw there's not a lot of hope. And a long, tough road in rehab. I'm not sure she has it in her. I wish she would go peacefully in her sleep tonight. That may sound harsh, but I don't think she'd want to live this way. Ultimately, it doesn't matter what I think or hope. Whatever will happen will happen.

It makes me fear getting older. Does she know what's happening? Does she remember that I was there? Are there more strokes to come? The nurse said some patients with dementia forget about the stroke incident. I'm supposed to be in Palm Springs on Thursday for my *Evening on the Lanai* show at Oscar's. And we sold out. What do I do? Will there even be anything for me to do here? Will she have to be moved to a rehab facility? So many questions. Now sleep. If I can.

I decided to go do my *Golden Girls* Q&A show in Palm Springs. Taking a cue from Bea Arthur, who insisted we film the "Blanche &

The Younger Man" episode even though her mother had just passed, I knew my show must go on. I also didn't want to let the fans down. But I couldn't tell anyone, including Alexander Rodriguez, the host of the show.

I left a day later, after one more visit to the hospital. No change. My mom still wasn't eating or able to speak words that made sense. She was mostly sleeping. I drove out to Palm Springs, hoping a change of scenery would do me good. My blood pressure was elevated, I wasn't sleeping, and I was afraid I'd have a heart attack.

MAY 28, 2021   JOURNAL ENTRY

Sitting on my little deck at Saguaro Hotel in
Palm Springs looking at the beautiful moun-
tains. Tough morning after a great evening
at my *Golden Girls* show. But then woke up at
4 a.m., saw a long text from my sister about
where we're at with my mom. It doesn't look
good. She's had no improvement since Sunday
and keeps pulling the feeding tube out of her
nose. She'll be discharged today and go back
to Belmont but now under hospice care. No idea
how long she has to live. I can't believe I'm
writing these words. We've been together my
whole life. I don't know if I want to live in
a world without her. I'm going to get on the
road soon. Head back to God knows what. Going
straight to the hospital.

My mom never regained her comprehension, speech, or ability to swallow. At least she'd be back in her own room, surrounded by all her belongings. And under twenty-four-hour care. I was hoping she'd start eating again. Regain some strength. Maybe talk. We always joked that she'd live to be 101, like my grandmother. But those were the most painful days for me. Having her grip my hand tight and mumble, "Help me." To die or to live? I didn't know. She was still pulling out the tube that was giving her air and feeding her. Why wasn't she getting better?

MAY 30, 2021   JOURNAL ENTRY

Just hung up with Rande and started crying
again. Then I said out loud to myself, "Why
does this hurt so much?" I don't know the
answer to that. I knew this day would come. I
saw her health declining. But otherwise, she
was strong. This has been such an emotional
rollercoaster. Just when it seems like she is
done, she'll say "Hi" back or hold my hand.
Tonight, nothing. I don't know if it's the
medicine (or morphine), or her body is just
shutting down. I feel so helpless. But I know
we did all we could. She got the best care. Yet
here we are. I love her SOOOOO much it literally hurts. I don't care if people call me a
"Mama's Boy." I wear that title with honor. I
wonder if I'll run out of tears. Probably not.
She never ran out of love for me.

MAY 31, 2021   JOURNAL ENTRY

My mom could pass at any moment. This is it.
I walked to Belmont from my house today. I
said my good-byes. I've said them many times
over the past week. It's so draining going
there. Even the hospice worker told me to go
home. She thought I was too emotional a person
to sit there all day. I feel guilty that I'm
not going back tonight. But why? My mom knows
how I feel. What if showing up gives her some
sense that she needs to hang on?

These have been the hardest days of my life.
When I saw Liz Torres in the dining room last

night, we grabbed each other's hands and started crying.

She softly pleaded with me, "Please, don't leave me."

I promised her I wouldn't.

Liz then said, "Valerie Harper told me that losing a mother is the hardest thing you'll ever have to do."

So true. A mother is the one person who loves you unconditionally. Or at least that's the relationship my mom and I had.

A friend said that you have to make sure you say four things:

I love you.

Thank you.

I apologize.

I forgive you.

How amazing that with my mom, I only had to say the first two. We had such a unique relationship. I've cried so many times this week. In front of people and on the phone. To Peter, Rande, Adrienne. The staff at Belmont, who really loved her. Marlene at the front desk. I can't believe one of the PALS at Belmont, Lisa Schulman, came in on her day off just to sit with my mom. Susanne was a charmer. And very funny. I must've gotten my sense of humor from her. And so much more. Mine is much rosier than hers. But that same sense of practicality. It is what it is. And, you just deal with it. And now she's dealing with her end of life. And I must as well. She'll always be with me. And luckily through my words, on and on.

When I was crying with my sister the other day
on the phone, I told her that I felt all alone
now. She said I wasn't. I said, "You have your
family. I have no one."

JUNE 1, 2021   JOURNAL ENTRY

Another roller coaster day. Thank God my sister finally arrived. I could've sworn my mom
had a tear in her eye when my sister and I
were standing together by her bedside. This
has really been the most painful experience of
my life. Seeing my mom, who sacrificed so much
for me, in that state and not being able to do
anything. I guess I shouldn't say that. I've
done so much for her. And now I'm helping her
transition. She told me so many times that she
would not want to live in a compromised state.
Which she has been for years.

The night my sister was leaving, my mom opened her eyes. She didn't really look at us, but we knew she heard us. I let my sister have a moment alone with her, even though she said she didn't need it.

The next day, I was planning to visit my mom after lunch, but Peter Golden suggested I go in the morning. I did. I asked the hospice nurse to leave the room, so I could have a private moment with my mother. I sat next to her and cried like I've never cried.

Then I said, "I know this is going to sound really corny, and I can't believe I'm going to say this out loud, but if you see the 'white light,' it's okay to go toward it. Rod and your parents, and our little dog Toto, will be there waiting for you. And don't worry, I'll be alright."

An hour and a half later . . .

JUNE 4, 2021   JOURNAL ENTRY

At 1:32 p.m. PST, my mom passed. From the time of her stroke to her death was thirteen days. Might not seem important to anyone but me. The 13th is my birthday, my Bar Mitzvah was on the 13th, and for years it's a number that keeps popping up. Was the world preparing me for that amount of time?

What a rough week it was. Mostly for me. I hope not for her. But it all played out perfectly in a weird, cosmic way. I think my mom waited until my sister left and to have one last time alone with me. I thanked her again and again. Said how much I loved her. And not a day will go by that I won't think of her. She meant EVERYTHING to me. I was SO lucky to have her as a mother. As my biggest cheerleader. And best friend. She made me promise to never leave her. And I didn't. I reminded her of that. I walked her back home. I think that's why she felt she could finally leave this earth. I'm so grateful for that moment. For all the moments we had together. But I'm exhausted. What a wild thirteen days. I feel relieved. But also very, very sad. I will miss her, even though with her dementia, I lost her years ago.

I seem to be losing so many important women to me. I must find strength from their strength. And really start to rebuild my life now. This can be an exciting new chapter. But I have to fly. Live each day to its fullest. So many possibilities. All due to the most important woman in my life. MY Golden Girl. My mom.

After my mom passed, I kept my promise and still visit Liz Torres every other Monday when I'm in town. Some people think that's odd. I won't lie. There is a part that is really tough to go back to Belmont. I keep thinking my mom will come around the corner with her walker and smile that big smile she always had upon seeing me. But that will never happen.

When my first play was published in August of 2021, just a few weeks after we buried my mom, I knew what I had to do. I wrapped up the newly bound script, put it in a gift bag with a colorful bow, and went over to see Liz. Her face when opening it was priceless. She understood exactly what that meant to me. And my mom. And everything my mother had done to get me to that day.

Below is what I posted on Facebook/Instagram about my mother's passing. The hardest part was hitting the "Share" button. That would mean it was final. More tears. And then I did it.

What happened next shocked and overwhelmed me. Over 900 people "reacted" to my post, and over 600 left a comment, not to mention countless texts, DMs, emails, cards, flowers, and food. The messages that touched me most were from mothers with young sons. They expressed how they hoped that *their* sons would grow up and feel as deeply for them as I did for my mother.

Here's the post, which was accompanied by a picture of how I want to remember my mom, sitting on the deck of my Laguna Beach rental, her eyes glistening as much as the Pacific Ocean behind her:

I will never love another person as much as I loved this one. And not just because she gave me life. But also because she taught me how to live it. And how to dream big. And once I told her my dreams, she supported me with every fiber of her being. I am me because of her. I may be a writer by trade, but my most important job has always been as a "son." Hopefully a good one. You can now rest peacefully, Mom. Love you to the moon and back.

The End (for now...)

‹

IMAGES

HEAR YE, HEAR YE, HEAR YE!

1) Cranbrook Theatre School used my photo as "The Herald" in "12 Dancing Princesses" for their official Christmas card. I was honored.

2) I was obsessed with Lily Tomlin as a kid. I made my mom take me to Northland Shopping Mall in Detroit to get her to sign my copy of her first comedy LP.

3) For our 13th birthdays, our parents offered us a trip anywhere in the world. You can see which city I picked - Hollywood!

4) I have to say I made a really good Scarecrow in
the summer stock production of "The Wizard of Oz" at
Hampton Playhouse (Hampton, New Hampshire).

5) Me dancing as "Dream Albert" in my high school's
production of "Bye Bye Birdie", which I also choreographed. My friend Adrienne Gornstein, is behind me
as "Anita".

6) My first headshot. I can't believe I had that much
hair. And it was that curly naturally.

7) Me and Rande Leaman dressed as geeky characters
(Guy & Lil) to welcome freshman at our NYU dorm,
Brittany Hall, during our sophomore year.

8) In my dressing room at the Mark Hellinger Theatre, in costume as an old Russian teacher. I made my Broadway debut in "Nureyev & the Joffrey Ballet".

9) My mom and me at my NYU graduadon in Washington Square Park.

10) My first solo apartment on W. 15th Street in Chelsea in NYC. It was a fifth floor walk-up. Notice the two burners on the half fridge. And dial phone on one of the first answering machines. I was very fancy.

11) Me and Jim as extras on the film "The Chosen". We worked on our scripts in between takes. Never a moment wasted.

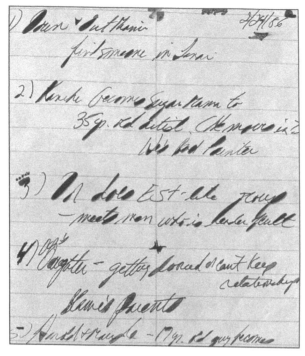

12) Here are some pitch notes while we were staff writers on "The Golden Girls". I wonder how many would have made good episodes. I'm sure a good therapist could analyze why I like to color in the circles.

13) Yes, I had a fro/mullet while writing on Season 1 of "The Golden Girls". Jim took this of me from his desk right across from me.

14) Rue McClanahan was so sweet to drop by our table to wish us luck when we were nominated for a WGA Award for our "Blanche & the Younger Man" episode. The ladies were presenters that night. Estelle said she stayed until our category.

15) Of course, the first house I bought had this incredible view of the Hollywood Sign. The entire structure was on stilts. Not land. Which was not fun during the Northridge Earthquake.

16) Me and Jim looking dapper at Lance Loud's birthday party. Taken by the very talented Stephen Jerrome.

17) I took this "arty" black and white photo of my grandmother in her apartment. I had just interviewed her on videotape to get some of her stories down.

18) Jim and I holding Shirley Jones' Oscar for "Elmer Gantry". This pic is from a 4th of July party in Beverly Hills. Shirley wasn't home. Our friend Jhoni Marchinko was the assistant to Shirley and Marty Ingels. I did sneak upstairs so that I could say I was in Shaun Cassidy's bed.

19) Estelle Getty came to my 30th birthday party. She was that kind of person. She made the effort.

20) Singing legend Debbie Harry, me and Allee Willis at artist Andre Mirapolsky's birthday party. Another incredible shot by photographer Stephen Jerrome.

21) Me and my mom in the kitchen set of "Roseanne". She came down from Santa Barbara for many tapings. I begged her not to talk to John Goodman for fear of Roseanne's wrath.

22) The writing staff of "Roseanne" were required to purchase tickets to Roseanne's Roast at the Friar's Club in Beverly Hills. Here I am with Betsy Borns, Amy Sherman-Palladino, Jim Berg and Lois Bromfield.

23) The writing staff of "Roseanne" were not happy with Roseanne that day, so we took her framed photo down from the office wall and threw food at it to let out our aggression. Somehow, I ended up with the only evidence, this Polaroid.

24) Me and Jim watching Tom Arnold introduce us at
the GLAAD benefit in West Hollywood for the airing of
our "lesbian kiss" episode of "Roseanne". I'll never
forget the roar of the crowd when we all watched
Mariel Hemingway kiss Roseanne on the big screen.

25) Jim and I went to Nashville to talk country singing sensation K.T. Oslin into doing a sitcom. Here
we are in front of the Loveless Motel Restaurant.

26) I got to meet Hilary Clinton at a morning backyard LGBTQ fundraiser in the Hollywood Hills when
she was first running for Senator from New York.
I'll never forget how eloquently she spoke without
notes or anything prepared.

27) Jim in our "closet" office on the Paramount lot
writing "The Brady Bunch Movie".

28) Me and Jim with Christne Taylor (Marcia Brady) on the set of "The Brady Bunch Movie". at Paramount Studios in Hollywood. She was so brilliant we kept writing more lines for her.

29) Jim, Producer Jenno Topping, me and Director Betty Thomas on the famous Brady stairs on set at Paramount Studios during the filming of the first film.

30) Jim, Priscilla Presley and me outside the Beauty Shop Restaurant in Memphis. We were on a research trip while writing a musical play about her life. We surprised her by telling her to meet us there, which was originally where she got her beehive hairdos done back in the day.

31) I made a collage of Lauren Graham on the back of our office door on "Gilmore Girls". She never knew I did this. I'm sure she would've called Security.

32) Lauren Graham came out to support me for the Opening Night Party in Hollywood of my Bravo reality show "Situation: Comedy" produced by Sean Hayes.

33) Me, Nicole Sullivan and Jim at the upfronts for our Lifetime sitcom, "Rita Rocks".

34) My friend Julie (Silverman) Sachse giving one of the best Christmas gifts ever, wood coasters of the Golden Girls!

35) Whoopi Goldberg backstage at NYC's Signature Theatre after a performance of "It's On!", my TV theme song musical

36) The cast of "Hot in Cleveland" (and some other very talented actors) did a benefit reading of our "Blanche & the Younger Man" script from "Golden Girls" for Celebration Theatre. I did not want the night to end. Talk about a full circle moment.

37) Me and Vanessa Williams at a big benefit reading of "Right Before I Go.", my suicide notes play. She was host for the evening at NYC's Town Hall. I would later act opposite her in an online reading during Covid.

38) Publicity pic of me and Sandra Bernhard taken for our Tellofilms webseries "Secs & Execs". Photo by Nathalie Taylor.

39) I was so proud to get Mindy Sterling her first
Emmy nomination for her performance in our webseries, "Secs & Execs". What a fun event!

40) The first time I appeared on Brooke Baldwin's CNN show, "Newsroom". I wore my infamous "#13" t-shirt that Tom Arnold and Roseanne gave the writer staff so that they wouldn't have to fire us by name. I was on the show LIVE to talk about Roseanne's firing and her comments about Valerie Jarrett, senior adviser to Barack Obama.

41) Me on one of many visits to see Liz Torres, "Miss Patty" from "Gilmore Girls".

ABOUT THE AUTHOR

Stan Zimmerman is a man of many mediums (TV, film, and theater). He's been nominated for two WGA Awards for Best Comedy Episodic Writing on the classic TV series *The Golden Girls* and *Roseanne*. Stan has also written and produced on *Gilmore Girls*, co-created the Lifetime sitcom, *Rita Rocks*, and wrote on both Brady Bunch movies. Stan has a BFA in Drama from NYU/Circle in the Square and has directed such LA productions as *Entertaining Mr. Sloane*, *A Tuna Christmas*, *Gemini*, *Pledge*, *Heartbreak Help*, and his original plays—*Meet & Greet*, *Knife to the Heart*, and *Have a Good One*. Stan appeared on Broadway with *Nureyev & the Joffrey Ballet* and in an East Coast tour of his suicide awareness play, *right before I go*, with Virginia Madsen and *Gilmore Girls* cast members. He was the Host/Showrunner on Sean Hayes's Bravo reality show *Situation: Comedy* and has been seen numerous times on CNN. Stan directed Colin Mochrie (*Whose Line Is It Anyway?*) in Hyprov (Daryl Roth Theatre). TRW Plays recently published and licensed three of Stan's works—*Yes, Virginia, Silver Foxes, and right before I go*. *Silver Foxes*, directed by Michael Urie, had its world premiere at Dallas's Uptown Players in March 2023.

Milton Keynes UK
Ingram Content Group UK Ltd.
UKHW020649040324
438885UK00017B/979

9 781954 676602